Working Smarter

Getting more done with less effort, time and stress

Viva Books
New Delhi | Mumbai | Chennai | Kolkata
Bangalore | Hyderabad | Kochi | Guwahati

First Indian Edition 2009

VIVA BOOKS PRIVATE LIMITED

- 4737/23 Ansari Road, Daryaganj, New Delhi 110 002
  E-mail: vivadelhi@vivagroupindia.net, Tel. 42242200
- 76, Service Industries, Shirvane, Sector 1, Nerul, Navi Mumbai 400 706
  E-mail: vivamumbai@vivagroupindia.net, Tel. 27721273, 27721274
- Jamals Fazal Chambers, 26 Greams Road, Chennai 600 006
  E-mail: vivachennai@vivagroupindia.net, Tel. 28290304, 28294241
- B-103, Jindal Towers, 21/1A/3 Darga Road, Kolkata 700 017
  E-mail: vivakolkata@vivagroupindia.net, Tel. 22836381, 22816713
- 7, Sovereign Park Apartments, 56-58, K. R. Road, Basavanagudi, Bangalore 560 004
  E-mail: vivabangalore@vivagroupindia.net, Tel. 26607409, 26607410
- 101-102 Mughal Marc Apartments, 3-4-637 to 641, Narayanguda, Hyderabad 500 029
  E-mail: vivahyderabad@vivagroupindia.net, Tel. 27564481, 27564482
- First Floor, Beevi Towers, SRM Road, Kaloor, Kochi 682 018, Kerala
  E-mail: vivakochi@vivagroupindia.net, Tel: 0484-2403055, 2403056
- H. No. 12, P. B. Road, Near Arya Hospital, Rehabari, Guwahati 781 008
  E-mail: vivaguwahati@vivagroupindia.net, Tel: 0361-2735624

www.vivagroupindia.com

Published by arrangement with

Thorogood Publishing
10-12, Rivington Street,
London EC2A 3DU

ISBN-10: 81-309-0381-4
ISBN-13: 978-81-309-0381-1

Published by Vinod Vasishtha for Viva Books Private Limited, 4737/23, Ansari Road, Daryaganj, New Delhi - 110 002.

Printed and bound by Sanat Printers, Kundli - 131 028, Haryana.

About the author

Graham Roberts-Phelps

Graham Roberts-Phelps is an international specialist consultant in business and personal development, sharing his ideas and insights with thousands of people and organisations every year. With an extensive background in management and business development, Graham works with organisations of many different types and sizes. Today, as a Director of 80/20 Training Ltd, professional speaker and consultant, prolific author, and a busy family man, Graham certainly 'walks the talk', carefully balancing his time and energy between these activities.

Take a tip...

Throughout the book, handy **tips** relevant to the text will be displayed in the footsteps illustrated here.

Draw on your initiative!

A pen or pencil will be useful when you complete numerous questionnaires, action plans and tests.

Relax!
Put your feet up. Handy **TIP** boxes will make your life easier!

Remember!
Make your own notes – add ideas, highlight or mark passages that you might want to review later.

Contents

1. Introduction to Working Smarter 1

Stop working harder – work smarter 2
Golden rules for Working Smarter 5
Live in the real world 6
Time management equals choice management 8
Tips for more effective personal time management 11
Good time management is an attitude 14
So what is the right attitude? 15
Beliefs and feelings about time 16
Why we waste time 20
Personal time effectiveness self-assessment 22
How people manage time differently 23
Which approach is best? 28
How to balance your work style 30
Summary 34

2. Plan the work and work the plan 39

Do your thinking on paper 40
Focus on your key performance indicators 41
Set monthly goals and objectives 43
Creating a daily action plan 45
A time management system that works! 47
Allow for uncontrollable time 50
Batch tasks together 50
Plan your week in advance 51
Applying the 80/20 rule 52
The night before list 59
The sixty-four thousand dollar question 59
First things first 60

3. How to gain one hour a day – every day 61

Learn to know where your time goes 62
Expect the unexpected 64
Create a non-interruption zone (NIZ) 65
Dump trivia 65
Do less and achieve more – delegation 66
Anticipate and look for opportunity time 68
Speed up routine tasks 69
Stop doing other people's work 70
Concentration of power 70
Clean up your communications 71

4. Positive goal setting 75

The importance of goal setting 76
Understanding how goals work 77
Setting S.M.A.R.T goals 78
How to set goals 79
Review goals regularly 80
An introduction to goal setting 82
Seven steps to goal achievement 85
Steps to your goals 87
Using behaviour modification principles 89
Create more balance in your life 93
Self-recording as a tool for self-development 94

5. Dealing with office interruptions 101

Why people interrupt you... 102
How to say 'NOT NOW' nicely 104
Creating the right environment 104
Using non-verbal signals 107
How to become more assertive 108

Assertive techniques 111
Verbal assertion 111
Types of assertion – summary 115
No more nice guy! 116
Avoid interruptions 118
How to say 'NO' nicely 119
Learn to negotiate timescales 122
Dealing with your boss 123
Ruthless with time, gracious with people 124

6. Dealing with telephone interruptions 125

Don't ask people to call you back 126
Give call back times 128
Batch calls together 129
Preparing for effective telephone conversations 130
Make notes when you are on the telephone 132
Stand up whilst you are making telephone calls 132
Time your telephone calls 133
Use a call divert for one hour a day 134
Screen calls effectively 135
Further application points 136

7. Conquering the paperwork battle 139

When in doubt – throw it out 140
Keep a clear desk 142
Dejunk your desk 143
Fantastic filing 144
The ten commandments of e-mail 145
Improve note taking with mind maps 146
Active reading 149
Knowing what you want to know 150
Improving reading speed 154
SQ3R: Survey, Question, Read, Recall and Review 158
Communicate information quickly and effectively 159
Efficient proof-reading 162

8. Overcoming procrastination 165

Why do we resist change? 166
How to stop procrastination 168
Techniques to manage procrastination 173
Seven day procrastination plan 175
Procrastination: Ten ways to 'do it NOW' 177

9. Working smarter for managers 181

Work to precise and measured objectives 182
Setting department result objectives 183
Setting objectives for you 188
Review activity 189
Planning your time 191
Working smarter as a manager 192
Keeping a weekly time management log 195
Managing committed and usable time 197
Planning your time 198
Types of management activity 201
The first step: Diary keeping 205
Managing versus troubleshooting 207
Delegation for managers 210
Be a proactive time manager 214
Reactors versus planners 216
Time management for managers – summary 220

10. Miscellaneous tips and ideas 227

Working in a 'virtual office' 228
Working at home 229
Ideas for successful motoring 233
Ideas for successful travelling – hotels 234
Ideas for successful travelling – airlines 235
Career development 236
Action learning and learning to learn 237
Using a log book for action learning 239
Career planning in a time of change 241

11. Managing stress and anxiety 249

BEWARE...! 250
Introduction to stress management 250
Stress and anxiety management 254
How to relieve stress at work 256
Avoiding burn-out 259
Handling depression 262
Optimum stress levels 264
Eliminating stress from your environment 269
Anxiety 272
Stress reduction techniques 273
Some healthful hints 274
And finally... 279

Introduction to Working Smarter

Stop working harder – work smarter: Has technology failed us?

Golden rules for Working Smarter: What is Working Smarter? • Finding your own golden rules

Live in the real world

Time management equals choice management: How to make better choices regarding the use of your time Goal setting

Tips for more effective personal time management: Spend time planning and organising • Set goals • Prioritise Use a to-do list • Be flexible • Consider your biological prime time • Do the right thing right • Eliminate the urgent Practice the art of intelligent neglect • Avoid being a perfectionist • Conquer procrastination • Learn to say 'NO' Reward yourself

Good time management is an attitude

So what is the right attitude? The importance of taking more control

Beliefs and feelings about time: Answers • Key principles

Why we waste time: Time stealers

Personal time effectiveness self-assessment: Time bandits

How people manage time differently: Directors • Instigators • Relaters Planners

Which approach is best? Director Instigator • Relater • Planner

How to balance your work style: **The** director • The instigator • The relater The planner

Summary

Stop working harder – work smarter: Has technology failed us?

Golden rules for Working Smarter: What is Working Smarter? • Finding your own golden rules

Live in the real world

Time

one

Stop working harder – work smarter

Over the last 15 to 20 years there has been an expectation that the world of work should be getting easier not harder.

Has technology failed us?

The promise of the personal computer age was to create the 'paperless office'. The introduction of more sophisticated and larger motorway networks, the expansion and privatisation of many public transport systems, the introduction of fax machines, e-mail, Internet and mobile 'phones have all raised the expectation of being able to do more with less effort and less time. The reality however is starkly different from this.

Travel...

- Business people and commuters today travel more than they ever have done.
- The supposed age of technology that should enable us to work from anywhere in the world has not yet happened.
- Instead, everyday millions of people sit in traffic jams or crowded trains in order to get to work.
- The average speed of traffic in London is seven miles an hour. This is slower than the horse and carriage of 100 years ago.
- The improvement in air travel means that business executives fly from country to country every few days. Even in our leisure time we expose ourselves to the stress and vigour of increased travel.

Information...

The information flow that confronts most of us on any typical day is quite daunting. We now spend more time producing paperwork than ever before, despite e-mail and personal computers. Technology now enables us to endlessly edit letters and reports.

A typical manager or executive returning to his or her desk after a day away from the office may find 30 or 40 e-mail messages waiting. It is not uncommon for people to be constantly distracted by the ever-increasing crescendo of blips announcing the arrival of yet another carefully sent e-mail message.

Personal control...

The culmination of this is a world where we increasingly feel little control over our daily lives and activities. Survey after survey, in virtually every developed economy, highlights the fact that people feel that work is running them, not the other way around. The image of the hard-pressed executive feeling guilty by trying to balance time between family commitments and work is now almost a cliché except for the fact that it is true.

Unlike previous generations, where perhaps the pressure for long working hours was one of necessity born out by gruelling hours in low paid work, today we simply *aspire* rather than *require* things that we work for. The lure of a new BMW is what drives us to work endless hours, rather than a need to put food on the table.

Recognising this is one of the key elements to Working Smarter. There is nobody else that can create time for you other than you. It's not going to just happen. *The only person that really cares about how you balance your life is you.*

Companies, organisations, whether private or public, well or badly run, will happily take every last minute that you will devote to it and use it to their advantage. This is not to say they are heartless or uncaring, instead they will reward you and recognise you, but at the same time realise that you may do so at your own volition.

Longer hours and less job security

1. Many organisations, either consciously or unconsciously, generate an environment of insecurity and internal competition.

2. Managers, employees and professionals feel driven to do a good job and be seen working hard and competing well against each other.

3. In Japanese and American companies a culture can exist of not wanting to be seen to leave the office first. This becomes an almost self-fulfilling and self-perpetuating trend.

4. People do not take lunch – they simply grab a sandwich and carry on working.

5. Bars and cafés are increasingly full of people trying to eat, make notes and juggle their mobile 'phone all at the same time.

This continual whirlwind of business and activity is largely unsustainable. Medical professionals and researchers have long identified Type A behaviour as the drive and desire to constantly achieve higher and higher tasks and goals. This desire to please and achieve often creates people who skim, skip and rush, dash, and create stress-filled lives.

The term 'Type A' derives from a study conducted in American hospitals when personality types of various heart attack victims and their lifestyles were analysed. It was noticed that there was a correlation between the people who had heart attacks most commonly and the way they lived their lives. The people that had heart attacks *less* frequently were labelled as Type B. Those beginning to fill the wards with heart attacks, strokes and coronary problems were more commonly Type A behaviour. In a world where we seem to have invented a cure for most diseases in the modern world, with two notable exceptions, the fact is we don't die, we kill ourselves. A Forbes survey in 1991 highlighted the fact that nearly 80 per cent of the wealth in America is owned by women over 40. Most of the men who slaved 18 to 20 hours a day to achieve their great wealth and achievement did not live long enough to enjoy it. The survey also predicted that most of those women will probably spend the money before they died. And who can blame them?

Golden rules for Working Smarter

What is Working Smarter?

Working Smarter is about approaching your life, work and goals in a more sustainable, enjoyable and less stressful way than any other method.

It can be used with almost any diary system or time management planner. Working Smarter is a refreshing new approach, a new model, and a new philosophy which guides you into making the everyday decisions which affect your enjoyment and your future.

In arriving at this new way of working, you must be prepared to make some hard decisions and do some tough talking to yourself about what you really want to have, be or do.

In order to begin Working Smarter you need to:

- Set priorities using the 80/20 rule – selecting the critical few tasks and activities from the trivial many
- Plan the work and then work the plan
- Avoid routinely taking work home and staying late
- Be selective, always. Throw away or discard everything you can live without
- Do jobs requiring mental effort when you are at your best
- Do one thing at a time
- Establish a fixed daily routine
- Establish realistic working goals
- Fix deadlines for all jobs and stick to them

- Learn to say 'No', 'Not now' or 'Here's how you can do it'
- Make a regular check on your use of time
- Never postpone important matters that are unpleasant
- Occasionally, analyse your interruptions
- Plan your telephone calls whenever possible
- Put off everything that is not important
- Set a definite time or meetings to discuss routine matters
- Treat a large job as a series of small, achievable tasks.

Beware that the very simplicity of some of these ideas does not hide their effectiveness. Achievement in important tasks and goals is highly stimulating. While you obviously feel tired after a good day achieving results, it will be quite a different feeling from the frustration you experience when you are continually prevented from turning plans into action.

Finding your own golden rules

There are no easy answers to the management of time, but two factors are clear:

- Your own personal commitment is vital.
- Your attitude must be positive.

If both these conditions exist, a proper system can be implemented to ensure continuity of effort. An effective system should include certain golden rules to ensure that everybody can work in a planned and controlled way, not working from crisis to crisis or constantly 'running to stand still'.

Live in the real world

There simply is not enough time to do everything. We all know this is true, and yet our behaviour at work often suggests that we believe there actually is time to do everything. That is the case when we do the quick, the easy, the interesting, the fun and the enjoyable regardless of their urgency and importance. Not only is there not enough time to do everything, but also, not all of the time we have is controllable. Some of it is uncontrollable in that the time is not available to work on actions from our To-do list.

Time is the inexplicable raw material of everything. With it, all is possible, without it, nothing.

It is yours. It is the most precious of possessions.

We shall never have any more time. We have, and we have always had, all the time there is.

This is very good advice. Sometimes we look at a big project and don't know where to get started. An old Chinese proverb states that a trip of a thousand miles begins with the first step. Often when we take the first few steps the job looks smaller. Set out the things to be done in order of importance. Then, no matter how big the first item appears, jump right in and get started. This way, the only things you put off until tomorrow are the truly lesser things to be done. The important things will get done today.

If we are really careful of every minute in the day, it is amazing how many little minutes can add up. If we are determined to 'make time' to get things done that we want to do... we can do it. By keeping a time log, minute by minute, we will see where all those precious little minutes are leaking out of the bucket... until it is empty... the day is gone. Examine your time log carefully and you will discover what you need to do to have the extra time each day that you want.

To be effective time-managers we have to have direction and motion. Yes, we have to have a road-map... usually in the form of a To-do list. This provides us with the schedule of events to be done in order of importance. Once we have the 'road-map' (To-do list), we have to get into motion and... **GET THINGS DONE**! Effective time management is as simple... or as hard as that.

It is true of a great many people that given a five hour task and eight hours in which to complete it... the task will take eight hours. Many people stay busy all day long, but do not get very much done because they are allowing non-important work or details to use the time available. If we make a habit of timing each project and trying to get it to fit into a shorter time frame, we can usually do it.

Thus, have time to do other jobs that need doing. Sometimes it is very healthy to be pushed to complete a far greater quantity of work than before. If you are able to do it, you may find that some trivial things did not get done. Maybe these trivial little things should never get done... or at least done as a quick bunch job.

It is worth remembering that all of us are subject to Parkinson's Law – the notion that work expands to fill the time available for its completion.

Time management equals choice management

The phrase 'time management' is really a misnomer. The simple truth is that you cannot manage time. Time marches on and there is nothing any one of us can do to harness its swiftness. All of us, however, were born with a freedom to choose, and with these choices, we can manage and control what we **do** with our time.

If you are reasonably contented with your life so far, then you know you have made acceptable choices for the most part. If you are experiencing unrest, however, and never seem to have time for the things that are most important to you, start first with learning how to make better choices rather than trying, as most people do, to find more time.

How to make better choices regarding the use of your time

The first step is to identify the things that are most important to you. In other words, *start setting goals*. If you are not on your own goals program, you are on somebody else's. That somebody else could be a relative, a spouse, or an employer. Naturally, in a work environment, you will be given directives by a superior and will need to work within the framework set up by the employer. Most people, however, take this as a cue to relinquish all responsibility for themselves. Why are you working? What goals do you have for yourself that your job can help you accomplish? Answering these questions and creating a list of goals gives your work and your life new meaning.

Goal setting

Goal setting also creates compelling reasons to manage yourself better. Any choice you make regarding how to spend your time without the framework of important goals is usually made unconsciously and appears equally valuable. For example, watching television or reading the latest book on sales skills can appear to be equally good choices if no important purpose is attached to these activities. Now suppose your goal is to increase your sales results. Most likely, under this circumstance, you would choose to use your time reading the sales book because, in light of your sales goal, the choice to spend your time in front of the television doesn't help you get closer to achieving it. In short, creating a list of important objectives motivates you to analyse how to better use the limited amount of time you have.

Start listing goals today. Want to break a habit? List it. Want to change an aspect of your personality? List that too. Want to spend more time with your children? List that. Begin making a list today of all the things you would like to accomplish this week, this month, this year, next year.

The next step is to get a picture of how you spend time now. Quite often we create an illusion in our minds that we are very busy and do not have time for the things that are important to us. Once again, this is more a problem of not making decisions regarding what is important to you rather than not actually having the time. Your time picture will reveal those gaps of lost time that otherwise go unnoticed. Simply keep track of how you spend your time for one week. For example, 5.30-6.30 a.m. awoke, showered. 6.30-7.30 a.m. drive to work, etc. You may forget to record some items during the first few days but stick with it. This one exercise will make you very aware of how you currently choose to spend your time and may reveal opportunities to spend certain times, such as driving time, more productively.

This exercise ***must*** be done in relation to your list of goals. If you have no goals, the revelation that you spent an hour discussing your weekend won't give you any clues to becoming a better choice maker. In relation to your important goals, however, that hour may hold less meaning for you if that time could be better spent working toward a more meaningful end.

Finally, become a better choice maker at work. You were hired to perform certain tasks for your employer. Review your job description and identify those key activities that make use of your talents and abilities which are worthy of the rate of pay you receive to do your job.

Ask yourself these questions:

- What was I hired to do?
- What do I do that nobody else can do?

The answers to these questions are the keys to tasks that you should be spending the majority of your time on. For example, if your job is in sales, some of your key activities are to make appointments with potential clients. Many other duties you perform such as answering the phone, typing letters, etc., may not be key activities that will help you achieve what you were hired to do. Naturally, circumstances may demand that you do some less productive work, but do so consciously or delegate those tasks to another individual if possible. Adopt the same approach to your personal life.

Each goal that you set, will also have some identifiable key activities that will propel you quickly toward the achievement of that goal. Identify those activities, then staunchly guard and plan in the time necessary to accomplish them.

Throughout your day at work, at home, or any time you feel like you're out of control, ask yourself: '**Does what I am about to do get me closer to achieving the things that are important to me?**' The answer will start you on the path to making better choices for yourself and your family.

Tips for more effective personal time management

Spend time planning and organising

Using time to think and plan is time well spent. In fact, if you fail to take time for planning, you are, in effect, planning to fail. Organise in a way that makes sense to you. If you need colour and pictures, use a lot on your calendar or planning book. Some people need to have papers filed away; others get their creative energy from their piles. Organise ***your*** way.

Set goals

Goals give your life, and the way you spend your time, direction. When asked the secret to amassing such a fortune, one of the famous Hunt brothers from Texas replied: 'First you've got to decide what you want.' *Set goals which are specific, measurable, realistic and achievable.* Your optimum goals are those which cause you to 'stretch' but not 'break' as you strive for achievement. Goals can give creative people a much-needed sense of direction.

Prioritise

Use the 80-20 Rule originally stated by the Italian economist Vilfredo Pareto who noted that 80 per cent of the reward comes from 20 per cent of the effort. The trick to prioritising is to isolate and identify that valuable 20 per cent. Once identified, prioritise time to concentrate your work on those items with the greatest reward. Prioritise by colour, number or letter – whichever method makes the most sense to you. Flagging items with a deadline is another idea for helping you stick to your priorities.

Use a To-do list

Some people thrive using a daily To-do list which they construct either last thing the previous day or first thing in the morning. Such people may combine a To-do list with a calendar or schedule. Others prefer a 'running' To-do list which is continuously updated. Or, you may prefer a combination of the two. Whatever method works for you is best. Don't be afraid to try a new system – you just might find one that works even better than your present one!

Be flexible

Allow time for interruptions and distractions. Time management experts often suggest planning for just 50 per cent or less of one's time. With only 50 per cent of your time planned, you will have the flexibility to handle interruptions and the unplanned 'emergency.' When you expect to be interrupted, schedule routine tasks. Save (or make) larger blocks of time for your priorities. When interrupted, ask the crucial question to help you get back on track fast, 'What is the most important thing I can be doing with my time right now?'.

Consider your biological prime time

That's the time of day when you are at your best. Are you a 'morning person,' a 'night owl,' or a late afternoon 'whiz?' Knowing when your best time is and planning to use that time of day for your priorities (if possible) is effective time management.

Do the right thing right

Noted management expert, Peter Drucker, says 'Doing the right thing is more important than doing things right.' Doing the right thing is effectiveness; doing things right is efficiency. Focus first on effectiveness (identifying what is the right thing to do), then concentrate on efficiency (doing it right).

Eliminate the urgent

Urgent tasks have short-term consequences while important tasks are those with long-term, goal-related implications. Work towards reducing the urgent things you must do so you'll have time for your important priorities. Flagging or highlighting items on your To-do list or attaching a deadline to each item may help keep important items from becoming urgent emergencies.

Practice the art of intelligent neglect

Eliminate from your life trivial tasks or those tasks which do not have long-term consequences for you. Can you delegate or eliminate any tasks on your To-do list? Work on those tasks which you alone can do.

Avoid being a perfectionist

In the Malaysian culture, only the gods are considered capable of producing anything perfect. Whenever something is made, a flaw is left on purpose so the gods will not be offended. Yes, some things need to be closer to perfect than others, but perfectionism, paying unnecessary attention to detail, can be a form of procrastination.

Conquer procrastination

One technique to try is the 'Swiss cheese' method described by Alan Lakein. When you are avoiding something, break it into smaller tasks and do just one of the smaller tasks or set a timer and work on the big task for just 15 minutes. By doing a little at a time, eventually you'll reach a point where you'll want to finish.

Learn to say 'NO'

Such a small word – yet so hard to say. Focusing on your goals may help. Blocking time for important, but often not scheduled, priorities such as family and friends can also help. But first you must be convinced that you and your priorities are important – that seems to be the hardest part in learning to say '**NO**.' Once convinced of their importance, saying '**NO**' to the unimportant in life gets easier.

Reward yourself

Even for small successes, celebrate achievement of goals. Promise yourself a reward for completing each task, or finishing the total job. Then keep your promise to yourself and indulge in your reward. Doing so will help you maintain the necessary balance in life between work and play. As Ann McGee-Cooper says, 'If we learn to balance excellence in work with excellence in play, fun, and relaxation, our lives become happier, healthier, and a great deal more creative.'

Good time management is an attitude

In trying to understand more about why traditional approaches to managing our time often fails us, it is important to recognise one critical factor. Good time management is essentially an attitude. A way of thinking. A set of beliefs and values. Often people have all the diary systems, computerised planners, pocket organisers and so forth yet fail to make them connect in a way that positively allows them to get the most out of every day and week. Conversely, people who use none of those traditional tools are able to get a huge amount done and lead fairly normal and balanced lives by simply focusing themselves by using the right attitude.

So what is the right attitude?

The attitude that allows you to unlock your potential to get more done faster and easier than ever before is this: 'Value your time as if it was the most important resource that you have.' This means quite simply that you use every minute, second, hour and day as if it was the most important on earth.

The only thing we can really control with any certainty is the second that we now exist in. How many times have you heard people with grand plans that never come to much? How many times have you promised yourself to do something tomorrow, only to find that you haven't achieved it by the end of that day?

> **If you don't want to remind yourself about the importance of the attitude of good time management whenever you would use the word 'time' in the context of a sentence simply replace it with the word 'life'. So instead of saying 'What can I do with my time now?' you can say 'What can I do with my life now?' Instead of saying 'I am wasting my time' this would actually become 'I'm wasting my life.'**

The importance of taking more control

When you begin to take a little bit of control or a little more control, no matter how small, over some of the events in our day we can boost our productivity. If we have a few more minutes, we can get a few more things done. This in turn improves our self-esteem – how good we feel about ourselves, how confident we are and so on. We then improve our ability to be a little more assertive, forceful and confident in planning to take a few more elements of control over some of the events in the day. This will then improve our productivity, which will then boost our self-esteem, which then allows us to take a little more control, and this then

Ask yourself Townsend's[1] question a hundred times a day: 'Is what I am doing, or about to do, moving me towards my objectives?'

increases and the whole thing spirals to the point when you become almost unstoppable on the road to getting things done.

Do not be misled by the fact that some of the things you may want to start tomorrow are quite small. These are the first steps in the process. Just a few little changes, being a bit sharper on the telephone, not leaving messages for people to call you back and being a little more unavailable will allow you to begin the process of being more in control and being effective in the way that you manage your time.

Do not worry that they are little things, they do make a difference.

Beliefs and feelings about time

To highlight your own attitude towards time management, take this quick true and false test.

		True	False
1.	Unless the company is understaffed, people who use time wisely are normally able to find time for really important work activities.	☐	☐
2.	It is always best to wait until you have collected all of the relevant information and data before making a decision.	☐	☐
3.	In most jobs, people use their time in repetitive patterns that can be effectively analysed.	☐	☐
4.	You can achieve greater improvements in your use of time by analysing how you handle crises rather than how you go about your daily routine activities.	☐	☐
5.	The amount of time spent trying to achieve perfection is always time well spent.	☐	☐

(1) R Townsend, *Up the Organisation*, Coronet, 1970

	True	False
6. Good time management and being busy during the entire day are synonymous.	☐	☐
7. Most people already know exactly how they use their time.	☐	☐
8. The greatest time savings will normally come from preventing interruptions.	☐	☐
9. Frequent interruptions make setting priorities a rather unproductive drill.	☐	☐
10. Most people know exactly what their time management problems are.	☐	☐
11. Hard work is an effective substitute for good time management.	☐	☐
12. Time management techniques will turn you into a machine with no freedom to do the things you want to do.	☐	☐
13. In the short run teamwork and delegation to subordinates will invariably result in time savings for you.	☐	☐
14. How you manage your time will directly influence your effectiveness in supervising, communicating with and motivating your subordinates.	☐	☐
15. Most of the important results you achieve stem from only a handful of activities.	☐	☐

(Answers overleaf)

Answers

1. **TRUE**. You don't find time, you make it – we have all the time there is.

2. **FALSE**. Learn to use your intuition and wisdom to make smaller decisions and create time to analyse the fewer, more important decisions.

3. **TRUE**. We are all creations of our habits. Improving our time management means taking a conscious decision and expending effort to change the less effective habits to more effective ones.

4. **FALSE**. We waste hours doing many different smaller routine activities that take too long, distract us or should not be done at all.

5. **FALSE**. Perfectionism is a thief of time.

6. **FALSE**. It is more important to be effective, not efficient. There is no value in doing less important things well.

7. **FALSE**. Most people do not know exactly how they use their time.

8. **FALSE**. Often interruptions are part of the job that we can do little about. Customers are not interruptions.

9. **FALSE**. Frequent interruptions mean it is even more important to have a daily plan, not less.

10. **FALSE**. Most people don't know exactly what their time management problems are. They see their problems as things outside of themselves. Good time management is about effective self-management and applied self-discipline. This requires an open mind and a willingness to admit that we don't know or the answers need to change.

11. **FALSE**. Hard work is NOT an effective substitute for good time management; it leads to burn-out, stress and low self-esteem. Hard work does not make you more successful, it just makes you more tired.

12. **FALSE**. Time management techniques give you more time to be flexible and spontaneous.

13. **FALSE**. In the mid-long run, delegation and teamwork to subordinates will invariably result in time savings for you. This takes belief and patience.

14. **TRUE**. You cannot control other people's behaviours – only yours. So set an example.

15. **TRUE**. 80 per cent of our results come from 20 per cent of activities.

Key principles

1. You don't find time, you ***make*** it.
2. Learn to use your intuition and wisdom to make smaller decisions and create time to analyse fewer, more important decisions.
3. We are all creations of our habits. Improving our time management means taking a conscious decision and expending effort to change the less effective habits to more effective ones.
4. We waste hours in many different smaller routine activities that take too long, distract us or should not be done at all.
5. Perfectionism is a thief of time.
6. It is more important to be effective, not efficient. There is no value in doing less important things well.
7. Most people already know exactly how they use their time.
8. Often interruptions that we can do little about are part of the job. Customers are not interruptions.

Key principles *continued*

9. Frequent interruptions mean it is even ***more*** important to have a daily plan, not less.

10. Most people ***don't*** know exactly what their time management problems are. They see their problems as things outside of themselves. *Good time management is about effective self-management and applied self-discipline.*

11. Hard work is **NOT** an effective substitute for good time management; it leads to burn-out, stress and low self-esteem.

12. Time management techniques give you more time to be flexible and spontaneous.

13. In the short-term, delegation and teamwork to subordinates will invariably result in time savings for you.

14. You can't control other people's behaviours – only yours. So set an example.

15. 80 per cent of our results come from 20 per cent of activities.

Never do errands on impulse. Plan your route carefully, handling as many errands as possible each time.

Why we waste time

Time stealers

Time stealers are the most important obstacles that bar your way to achieving your objectives.

They may be your own fault, may be due to your surroundings or colleagues, or may even be of a psychological nature. The only way to deal with timestealers is to identify them. In some cases the problem may be outside your control, but if you know the cause it may reduce the negative effect on you. To identify timestealers draw up a list of the main obstacles which adversely effect your performance, together with possible solutions. Examples associated with the telephone might include:

- Discussion too lengthy: separate chat from information.
- Unstructured conversations: make a plan in advance.
- Unwanted calls get through: discuss the problem with your colleagues and make a plan.

Some areas where you are likely to find time stealers include:

- Poor meetings, poor communication.
- Poor delegation, unclear distribution of responsibility.
- Lack of priorities.
- Indecision and delay, crisis management.
- Lack of self-discipline, involved in too much.
- Too much paper work.
- Unplanned or uncontrolled interruptions.
- You may find that the vast majority of timestealers are of your own making. If this applies to you, you may have to change your attitude.
- It is most unlikely that you will change others; you can only change yourself.

Work on only **one** item at a time.

Personal time effectiveness self-assessment

Time bandits

Task: Take time to reflect on the ten time wasters listed below, ranking each in order of priority, or problems, in the space provided. Consider not only your experience in your current job, but in previous ones.

Time waster	Rank order
1. Face-to-face interruptions	
2. Lack of planning, goals and objectives	
3. Fire-fighting, crisis management	
4. Attempting too much	
5. Constantly shifting objectives	
6. Telephone interruptions	
7. Paperwork and personal disorganisation	
8. Inability to say 'no'	
9. Procrastination	
10. Lack of self-discipline	

When you have completed this exercise write your top three here:

1. ____________________

2. ____________________

3. ____________________

Now ask yourself – is there a link between them? If the answer is **YES**, then any improvement in one will automatically lead to an increased ability to overcome the other two.

How people manage time differently

In approaching this it is easy to make it sound more complicated than it usually is. In essence it is very simple. There are two major criteria to assess about yourself to try and understand how you can best organise your time and life. The first is a scale between being reactive and proactive (see below). Imagine a scale on a score of 1 to 4. At the left hand side of the scale no.1 you will be seen to be **reactive**. You much prefer to be involved in the planning rather than instigating or starting the planning process. Your daily routine activities will be taken up in responding to the work load calls or requirements of others. You are often happiest in this role. You find it easier to work constructively when others have assisted you in giving you direction, focus and work load. You will quite enjoy the buzz of having things happen which you have to deal with.

On the other end of the scale is **proactivity**. This is where you are perhaps not so happy or at ease with the constant and random series of events happening. You much prefer to be in control. You would prefer to be able to set your own tasks and goals without the interruption or distraction of other people.

Reactive — **Proactive**

1 — 2 — 3 — 4

The second element that will indicate your preferred style is your preference for working with tasks and things or people and persuasion (see over). At one end of the scale you will be A – very task focused, happier working on computers, machines, methodologies, paper-based systems and so on.

Your preferred way of working is probably to work quietly and calmly or methodically rather than have the constant buzz and interaction of people around you. You will enjoy company but in a planned way, rather than the random socialising and chatting that may often take place in other people's daily routine.

Tasks			People
A	B	C	D

At the end of this scale (D) you are very people oriented. You find yourself working best by bouncing ideas off other people. You need the constant interaction of other people in order to get concentrated, get things done and to enjoy what you do, and the people aspect is for you probably one of the most enjoyable parts of working in an office or organisation.

Assess yourself on each of these scales by putting a mark on the number or letter that you feel best represents you. You may also find it useful to complete the questionnaire on page 36, which will further allow you to identify your preferred working style.

Another way is to simply read the descriptions of the different works or organisations and styles below and ask yourself which one best represents you. It is important of course to remember that people are more varied and more complex than any simplified model can make them appear. So in reality many of us may vary in different aspects of our lives. For example, the person who is very organised at work may in their home life allow themselves more latitude and more room to be creative and perhaps a little less formal.

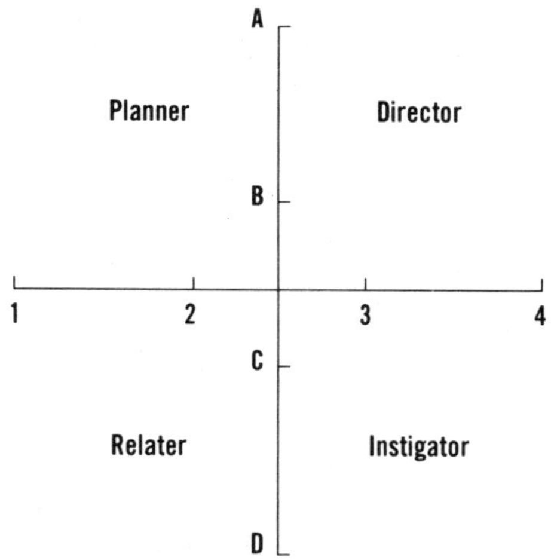

Here is a summary of the main four types of different self-management styles (illustrated above). See which particular approach you most identify with or best describes you in your day-to-day activities.

Directors

Directors combine the preference for task and results based activity with being keen to be proactive and in control. They are eminently practical in their approach and focused towards clear roles and objectives. Even without any clear objectives and roles their proactivity means that they will set these for themselves in the absence of others doing it for them. Very often they are self-motivated and self-directed. Their clear focus in results and achievement means that they will carry little baggage in terms of clutter, paperwork or sentimental items around them. In meetings they are clear and matter of fact, perhaps keeping 'small talk and partying' to a minimum.

The directors' style, and this refers to the way they work and not so much their job position, is one of almost workaholics. Their preoccupation with roles and results means that they strive constantly to achieve more. The only way they compete is either with themselves or for the recognition of being the best at what they do. Once they have achieved a certain plateau their proactivity means they set their sights on some new achievement or objective to gain.

In communication they are almost brisk and are often seen as being cold and difficult to deal with by some of the other styles, particularly the relaters and instigators.

Instigators

Instigators are very proactive, similar to directors. Instead of being driven by tasks and results they are driven more by the recognition and standing of other people. In contrast to directors they are very much more team players. They tend to be high energy individuals, able to generate enthusiasm in themselves and others. They communicate readily and easily, often expressing things other people think or feel. Their sense of enjoyment and fun with other people often means their communication is lengthy, with meetings taking longer than they might do, often because of the high element of social interaction and off-tangent discussion.

An instigator's strength is very often over the starting and literally instigation of key projects. It is at this point that their energy and enthusiasm is often at the highest. However, this is often their downfall because they are sometimes unable to complete or follow these projects through in the detail required because their enthusiasm sparks off another new project in the meantime.

Relaters

Relaters, like instigators, are very people oriented but unlike instigators they are much more reactive. They will not like to be seen necessarily as the centre of attention, a common trait of instigators. Instead, they will see themselves as mediators, counsellors, and friends. Whilst they may partake in the same level of communication as instigators they would do this in a different way. Their balanced and calm approach to problems and meetings allows them to see much more of a perspective than either instigators or the rather blinkered and sometimes over driven approach of directors. In some ways relaters are not motivated by goals, achievements or objectives at all. Their main motivation is often just the sheer enjoyment and interaction of other people's company. Indeed, many relaters will not see work or professional life as a primary goal at all.

To relaters perhaps the most important aspect to their life exists outside of work, and they do not need the achievement or recognition to give themselves fulfilment and satisfaction. Instead, the time and attention of friends and family is often far more important than anything they may appear to achieve in a professional capacity.

Relaters sometimes fail to be as proactive or as assertive as they should be – often not speaking up when they have ideas or leaving either directors or instigators to take the credit and the attention.

Planners

Planners on the other hand are reactive in the same or similar way to relaters but much more task focused rather than people focused. They will often balance the enthusiasm or the go-ahead drive of directors with a much more practical and pragmatic approach to seeing how things can be achieved. You often find planners managing projects, facilities or budgets. Their realism, logic and often extremely well organised and coherent approach means that their accuracy and thoroughness allows them a great deal of confidence in achieving things.

Whilst their approach may be seen to be rather cold and analytical by relaters and instigators and often seen to be too detailed and nit picky for directors, their clear desk and tidy mind approach is obviously a requirement in the kind of work that planners may do.

Which approach is best?

In considering each of these different general approaches to managing ourselves and our time, it should quickly become apparent that no one style is right. Instead each style will have their own distinct strengths and weaknesses. *The secret of Working Smarter is simply this: play to your strengths, do the things that you do best, but at the same time compensate carefully for the weaknesses which may prevent you from achieving all that you want to achieve.* Here are some examples:

Director

Strengths

- Goal centred
- Focused
- Results oriented
- Straight forward
- High work rate

Weaknesses

- Poor team-work
- Low people focus and consideration
- Failure to communicate things fully
- Inability to balance outside work interests, such as family or health

Instigator

Strengths

- High energy level
- Proactive and goal focused
- Good team player

- Natural motivater and persuader
- Easily able to motivate themselves
- High work rate
- Bags of enthusiasm

Weaknesses

- Lack of attention to detail
- Impatience in getting things done and started
- Inability to finish projects, procrastinating the final stages
- Often guilty of rushing in without careful planning, research or thought
- Tendency to over communicate

Relater

Strengths

- Strong people focus
- Able to relate to people and their emotions
- Able to listen, encourage and coach
- Practical in assessing and understanding situations and how best to react to them

Weaknesses

- Inability to motivate themselves
- Often suffer from procrastination, putting things off perhaps because of the fear of failure or the fear of criticism or rejection
- Lack of focus or goals, not as objective as they might be in assessing their own projects and capabilities
- Like to have a comfort zone around them or familiar objects
- Have a tendency to resist change and hoard their favourite tasks and resources
- They will take on far too much, possibly as a consequence of their reaction and reactivity and their desire to please others

Planner

Strengths

- High accuracy level
- Attention to detail
- Ability to plan and manage projects
- Personal organisation, filing and having a clear desk

Weaknesses

- Difficulty in relating or communicating projects or ideas with others
- Whilst considering the mechanical or logistical aspects they often miss the more people oriented aspects
- May also take on too much work with unrealistic deadlines. This is mainly because of their tendency for task focus and their preference for reactivity

How to balance your work style

Just in the same way there is no right or wrong style, there is no right or wrong way to manage your time. The best approach is to simply think carefully about your strengths and weaknesses. Maximise the things that you do best and at the same time work to control your weaknesses, so that they do not hold you back.

The following recommendations are provided as food for thought, but the only real test is if they work for you. When implementing any behavioural changes, it is important to allow yourself enough time to become familiar with the changes and to allow those changes to move from being conscious, deliberate actions into unconscious habits.

For example, if you are an instigator, or possibly a relater, one of your most common traits will be an untidy (or rather a very busy looking) desk. You will often have in-trays overflowing everywhere. In order to make sure that this weakness is not holding you back, you will perhaps need to move closer to the way of a planner or director works in this area, understanding of course that you may not want to become completely like them!

For the first two or three weeks this may seem rather odd and bizarre because it is not your normal way of working. However, once you begin to realise that the correct way is balance then you will realise it is worth making the effort.

The Chinese have an expression 'Moderation in all things.' Imagine seeing yourself through the eyes of somebody else. Imagine being a fly on the wall of your home or office and seeing how you go about your daily routine activities. What would you see? Could you improve? How could you manage to Work Smarter, achieving things more easily and more effectively?

This new 'Working Smarter' approach recognises several fundamental elements, often missing from other time management philosophies:

- There is no one right way of working. *It is simply what works for you.*
- What might be an outstanding strength for one person may, for someone else, simply be something they need to make sure they at least achieve the minimum. Directors or planners for example, will find having a clear well organised work area a definite asset in enabling them to get the most out of their day and life. For instigators and relaters, however, having a clear desk is simply a way of making sure that they avoid wasting time by looking for things or feeling out of control.

Here are some recommendations to consider.

The director

If this type of person best describes your approach you need to make sure that you still keep setting clear goals and objectives. Remember that not everybody works the way you do. Recognise that other people may see you as being cold, clinical and too autocratic. Try to balance this approach by taking time, even just a few minutes to interact with people, do things for the fun of it, discuss and build relationships with other people away from any goals or objectives.

Make sure that the goals and objectives on which you are working have clear action plans attached to them. This will ensure that you prepare carefully and do not invite unexpected obstacles or problems through lack of attention and planning.

It is also important to recognise the importance of balancing home, family, work and personal self-development and health aspects.

Plan each night what you are going to wear the next day, and lay it out ahead of time.

Doctors recommend that these type of individuals take up some form of exercise to balance their rather workaholic approach and burn off some of their stress and tension. When they do this, these individuals will usually take up a non-team based competitive sport such as golf, squash etc. This, whilst getting fresh air into the lungs and blood flowing through the muscles, will probably only perpetuate their goal orientation. Instead, take-up a hobby or a sport which is a complete contrast to your normal way of working. Not only will this provide a considerable change, doing something that you don't do naturally well, but also act as a suitable balance.

The instigator

Instigators have a variety of strengths including the humour, energy, enthusiasm and sheer momentum that they are able to generate in themselves and other people. In order to maximise this it is important to get a proper perspective when it comes to planning and attention to detail. Recognise that other people may find your energy and enthusiasm rather tiring and shallow. Try and build in times of quiet reflection. Sometimes the best thing that you can do is sit down quietly and think.

Make sure that your communication is clear. Build in regular times in your routine to catch up with the details that you often leave behind such as paper work, personal organisation, filing and so on. Whilst this will be a hard discipline it will be beneficial for you. Try not to take on too many tasks or objectives. Learn how to say no, particularly to your own ideas and put things into a realistic timescale to avoid conflicting goals. In essence, take time to plan and think things through before acting.

The relater

The relater's key strengths are being involved with people and relating to the way people work. In order to get the best out of your time it is important to balance this with slightly more objectivity and goal orientation. Aim to balance your obvious communication skills with some formal and practical planning and organisation. Take time every week to organise work through planning in advance and throwing things away. Spend time with directors or instigators. Your rapport and people skills will allow you to do this, although you may find mixing with these individuals rather hard work as their drive for results and progress may seem at odds with your view of people and relationships. Also, their striving for change and development may not sit too easily with your desire for consistency and order.

However, by mixing with directors and instigators you will see that they have strengths in the same way that they have obvious weaknesses. Take some of the things that they have strengths in and build at least an element of these into your day and work routine. For example, planning each day carefully on paper, working through agendas and project plans in meetings and setting clear deadlines and objectives in order to focus people and also motivate yourself.

The planner

The planners main asset is the retention of detailed analytical skills. Their sense of logic and pragmatism is a definite asset. However, occasionally this can often hold a planner back. To balance these strengths it is important to take time to look at the people aspects as much as the task and process at hand. Communicate regularly with the people involved.

Whilst this may need to be done constantly to start with and you may find other people's lack of attention to detail or rather, as you may see it, simplistic approach, rather difficult to adjust to, their energy of focus may help you balance the aspects of your work style. It also recognises that efficiency is not as important as effectiveness. For example, having a clear desk and well ordered filling system is not a goal in itself, it is simply a means to an end.

Make sure that you are not falling into the trap of perfectionism, striving to achieve excellence in things which are only there to serve as tools to achieve certain goals, objectives or make sure things happen. Avoid the tendency to over complicate documents or communicate things by setting clear deadlines and limits. Limit item agendas for example, and set time limits for meetings. Or, why not do something completely out of character, like join an aerobics class? By letting your hair down occasionally you will be able to focus more carefully and more intently on the strengths that you have that make you more effective.

Summary

In essence, the secret of Working Smarter is to actually have four approaches in one. To have four different styles of approach, to have four different personalities within each of us is the secret of getting the most done. There are times in the day, times in your life when you need to be goal oriented, focused and result centred. There are other times when you need to be a team player – motivational and persuasive – focused on people, and proactive. At other times the right approach would be calm and reflective

to make sure that you can walk out of the office early or on time to be with your family and friends and there are other times when careful checking and planning are essential.

Being able to switch between these different types of personality and balance one with the other as the situation demands is the key message in beginning to work smarter.

In managing your life and time well, you need to live your life and live each day like a tightrope walker. Every time you find yourself getting out of balance take a moment to catch yourself and realign with the trait or style that will bring you back in line.

Time management self-assessment worksheet

Complete the following questionnaire, as honestly and accurately as you can. Rate your response to each statement or question on the following scale:

(1) Never (2) Sometimes (3) Usually (4) Often (5) Always

1.	I start each day by reviewing or writing my daily schedule in writing	(1) (2) (3) (4) (5)
2.	I am able to easily set priorities based on my main goals	(1) (2) (3) (4) (5)
3.	I take time to plan ahead and regularly review my appointments and commitments	(1) (2) (3) (4) (5)
4.	I start work on the least favourite task first	(1) (2) (3) (4) (5)
5.	I am able to junk or delegate trivial tasks	(1) (2) (3) (4) (5)
6.	I avoid wasting time with interruptions and office socialising	(1) (2) (3) (4) (5)
7.	I arrive early for appointments, and allow for travel delays	(1) (2) (3) (4) (5)
8.	I don't waste time reading newspapers or magazines during prime work time	(1) (2) (3) (4) (5)
9.	I carry things with me that I can work on when I have a few minutes to spare	(1) (2) (3) (4) (5)
10.	I am able to delegate tasks easily and effectively	(1) (2) (3) (4) (5)
11.	I deal with paperwork as it arrives and use the principle of 'touch paper only once'	(1) (2) (3) (4) (5)
12.	I have an organised contact/message tracking system, and carefully log call-backs and notes on each contact	(1) (2) (3) (4) (5)
13.	I get reports done on time, and take time to analyse my results and effectiveness on a periodic basis	(1) (2) (3) (4) (5)

14.	I spend as much time as possible on important tasks before they become urgent	① ② ③ ④ ⑤
15.	I make time to exercise, relax or unwind regularly	① ② ③ ④ ⑤
16.	I feel in control of my daily routine and work schedule	① ② ③ ④ ⑤
17.	I never take on more than I can easily or comfortably accomplish	① ② ③ ④ ⑤
18.	I regularly set and review challenging goals for myself	① ② ③ ④ ⑤
19.	My work-rate is well above average for a normal day	① ② ③ ④ ⑤
20.	I invest in self-development time – books, tapes, seminars, new activities, etc.	① ② ③ ④ ⑤
21.	I know where my time goes	① ② ③ ④ ⑤
22.	I am realistic in making commitment for my time and others	① ② ③ ④ ⑤
23.	I throw away more than I file	① ② ③ ④ ⑤
24.	My filing system allows me to easily find things and I regularly have a clear out	① ② ③ ④ ⑤
25.	I maintain a daily sense of perspective and balance in my life	① ② ③ ④ ⑤

My score is _________ out of 25, or ______%.

- Score between 80 – 100%: **Excellent**.
- Score between 60 – 80%: **Very good**. A really high level of time management awareness.
- Score between 40% – 60%: **Good**. Room for improvement.
- Score less than 40%: **Poor**. What time do you get up in the mornings?

Plan the work and work the plan

Do your thinking on paper: Ideas to master each day

Focus on your key performance indicators: Key performance planning

Set monthly goals and objectives Monthly schedule

Create a daily action plan

A time management system that works! The three stage process • Daily schedule • Weekly schedule

Allow for uncontrollable time

Batch tasks together

Plan your week in advance

Applying the 80/20 rule: Pareto Analysis • Constructing a Pareto diagram • Setting priorities

The night before list

The sixty-four thousand dollar question

First things first

Do your thinking on paper: Ideas to master each day
Focus on your key performance indicators Key performance planning
Set monthly goals and objectives Monthly schedule
Create a daily action plan
A time management system that works! The three stage process • Daily schedule • Weekly schedule
Allow for uncontrollable time
Batch tasks together
Plan your week in advance
Applying the 80/20 rule: Pareto Analysis Constructing a Pareto diagram • Setting priorities
The night before list
The sixty-four thousand dollar question
First things first
Do your thinking on paper: Ideas to

two

Do your thinking on paper

If you get the **'I don't know where to start'** feeling – grab a piece of paper and brain-dump everything going through your mind. As well as helping you organise – it's good therapy.

Low technology but highly effective

A recent survey highlighted that less than a fifth of business and professional people actually make a written To-do list on an average day.

Whilst there might be many reasons for this, for example, not having enough time to make the list, feeling depressed or de-motivated when you see how many items there are to do on your list, or simply not having it defined as a routine or a habit, there is really no substitute for thinking on paper.

Frees mental thinking space

Writing things down frees the mind from having to try and remember what it is we should be doing. Many observers notice a similarity between the brain and our modern computer systems, and in managing your day better, writing to hard disk, or in this case paper, is definitely the way forward.

Get a permanent notebook

It is also important that when you develop the habit of thinking on paper, you do it in the form of a notebook. Thinking on bits of paper, or post-it notes, whilst better than no paper at all, is actually adding to the problem as well. You may well end up with two or three To-do lists, losing the To-do list, or not being able to follow it through in a rational way. By using a book you can actually refer back to the previous list, check items, remember telephone numbers, information, dates, times and so on.

Never put uncompleted activities from today at the top of tomorrow's To-do list. You must re-prioritise them.

Ideas to master each day

- Take ten minutes to make a note of important times, dates, projects and actions.
- Carry a notebook with you at all times – to capture all ideas, messages, records of telephone conversations, meeting actions, etc.
- Avoid using loose-leaf notes of sheets, these can be lost.
- Avoid using post-it notes or similar, these attach themselves to other documents and get lost more quickly, they can also encourage clutter thinking.
- To remove the stress out of solving a problem; write the problem clearly at the top of a page in the form of a question, and then brainstorm 20 ideas, no matter how crazy.

Focus on your key performance indicators

As we go through a day, as well as when we sit down and review our Action Plan and To-do lists in the morning, one of the key tasks we have to do is to make decisions about what is most important to be done. *This process of setting priorities is at the heart of all good time management and personal productivity.* However, in many cases, people make it harder for themselves to decide priorities by not having really clear objectives about their job, task or position. One thing that will definitely help you to deal with this is to take time out to discuss with your manager, supervisor or team leader what it is that is most important for you to achieve in your job or role.

How many times do you experience 'mind-blank' during the day, ie:

1. Walking into a room and forgetting why
2. Misplacing keys and personal effects
3. Losing names and telephone numbers.

Make time on a regular basis to review priorities with your manager/ team/partners.

These 'key performance indicators' will define the outputs of your job description, in priority, carefully highlighting the two or three aspects that are more important than all the others put together.

For example, the role of Credit Controller in a busy accounts department may entail a multitude of tasks. Clearly the over-riding outputs and objectives will be to reduce and manage overdue accounts. Once this is clarified, measures defined and the terms and order agreed, it can be a very valuable yardstick against which to set and manage priorities.

Key performance planning

Make some notes for each question or task.

Task 1

Using the 80/20 rule, list your top three or four outputs or performance indicators from your job.

Task 2

Write down three work-related projects, objectives or goals that you would like to complete in the next month or so.

Task 3

What are your greatest personal strengths, qualities or assets that you bring to your job and/or the organisation?

____

____

____

Set monthly goals and objectives

Another activity which is critical in being able to focus and deal with priorities successfully is knowing what your short-term objectives are for a period of time, say the next 30 to 60 days.

Whilst you may have some grand and long-term job outputs and objectives, a short-term goal and objective will allow you to focus successfully, gain a feeling of completion and progress and make it much more practical when it comes to deciding what to do and what not to do. For example, if you are a Sales Manager, you may have responsibilities for developing, coaching, generating sales, building new accounts, identifying new markets and so on. Trying to achieve all of these goals together will not only be frustrating, but also in the long run will not succeed. It is much better to select two or three significant goals for a particular month which will move you forward in key areas. Develop these into Action Plans and achieve them before moving on to other goals.

As well as setting daily and weekly Action Plans and schedules, it is also important to sit down once a month and ask yourself this question. *What are my three main goals or objectives for the next month*? Identifying these clearly, outlining Action Plans of how and when these can be achieved, will increase your ability to focus, to concentrate, to reduce distractions, to become more self-disciplined, and avoid you falling into the trap of trying to attempt too much. By limiting yourself to just three goals, you will invariably identify three important goals.

(*For more information on how to set goals see the following chapter.*)

Monthly schedule

month ______________

Day	Date	Activity
1		
2		
3		
4		
5		
6		
7		
8		
9		
10		
11		
12		
13		
14		
15		
16		
17		
18		
19		

20		
21		
22		
23		
24		
25		
26		
27		
28		
29		
30		
31		

Figure 1: A monthly schedule

Creating a daily action plan

Whilst I don't think anybody comes to work in the morning wanting to fail or achieve less than they could do, this is often a consequence because they fail to plan a proper daily schedule or Action Plan.

Without a plan we are left to the distractions, interruptions and ad hoc tasks that will pop up throughout the day. With a plan or schedule, when these interruptions and distractions occur, we not only have a good reason to deflect them (using our plan to justify why we cannot deal with things at that moment in time)

If you are always **'putting out fires'**, ask yourself after each crisis, (**a**) Why did it occur? (**b**) What can be done to prevent its recurrence? (**c**) If it does recur, how can I handle it better next time?

we can also know what to go back to working on after we have been interrupted or distracted.

If you have not done a schedule or daily plan before, this may seem rather strange and formal, however, there is no question that it is a key to effectively maximising your tasks. It makes it easier to become self-disciplined, it also makes it much easier to be realistic about what you can and cannot achieve during the day.

Assign time for anticipated activities that may happen – travel delays, ad hoc meetings, etc – live in the real world.

For example, in completing a daily schedule first thing in the morning you might quickly become aware that the amount of activities to be completed that day are fairly limited because of various things that are knocking out chunks of time, meetings, appointments and so on. It is much more advantageous to know this limitation at 9.05 than 5.05 when you realise that your aspirations to get a lot done have been frustrated. It will also be an opportunity to look at your plan and work load in advance and decide if there is an opportunity for delegation, dropping certain tasks and activities that are not really important, and checking the sequence of activities to make sure that you are doing first things first.

Typical daily and weekly schedules are shown in Figure 2 and 3 (see page 48-49). This is simply a timed plan for the day showing when you are actually going to be able to complete key activities and be available to others for interruptions, phone calls meetings and so on.

An alternative to trying to decide what your priorities are – decide what **NOT** to do first. Eliminate the less important and then prioritise a smaller list.

A time management system that works!

Instead of trying to decide what to do – first eliminate what **NOT** to do… filter out the trivia.

In studying extensively the various systems, approaches and methodologies to time management over the years, one thing becomes very apparent. Some systems work for some people and not for others, but no system seems to work for everybody.

The fact is that each and every one of us are completely unique individuals. For example, what about the person who is very detailed, analytical and organised methodically. How can they use the same system or approach time management in the same way as the person who is full of energy and bounding enthusiasm who leaves behind a trail of chaos. The two contrasting individuals are often found commonly working side by side.

In the eyes of one individual the other person is hopelessly disorganised. In the eyes of the other, the other person is simply so tied up with the process of planning it's a miracle they actually get anything done or finished at all. In studying people's different self management needs and approaches it soon becomes clear there are several distinct types of behaviour and approach to managing ourselves, our time and our personal organisation.

However, the following approach will work for nearly everyone. This is due to its flexibility and important underlying principles.

The three stage process

1. Scratchpad

- Do your thinking on paper, and make that paper a permanent notebook

2. Filter

- Sift, sort, cut out, discriminate, prioritise, filter

3. Action plan

- Work from a planned, realistic, sequenced and time bound action plan

Daily schedule

Today's most important goals:		
Schedule	Tasks and actions	Pr.
8am	**Call**	
9am		
10am		
11am	**Write**	
12 noon		
1pm		
2pm	**See**	
3pm		
4pm		
5pm	**Do**	
6pm		
Evening		

Notes:

Figure 2: A typical daily schedule form

Weekly schedule

date ______________

Day	This week's most important goals and objectives
Monday	
Tuesday	
Wednesday	
Thursday	
Friday	

Figure 3: A typical weekly schedule form

Allow for uncontrollable time

One important concept to consider and build into your daily planning process is the concept that you only have a certain amount of time which is controllable by you. This could be as much as 90 per cent controllable or only ten per cent controllable on a bad day or week. The things that take up our time could be boss imposed, task imposed by a manager or supervisor, things which are a regular or routine part of the job, and then there are customer driven interruptions.

For example, if you were a teacher in a school, giving classes to pupils is a routine part of the job that you would not delegate or not do because you have more important tasks. We put this time into the daily schedule first blocking out the key activities or allowing for the things which will generally happen but which we cannot control. Research and analysis shows that things we think are ad hoc, such as crisis management, interruptions by customers and so on will have a pattern and similarity to them.

This allows us to begin to plan and schedule time in anticipation for these things happening. For example, if you would estimate that you would have approximately two hours in total of customer driven interruptions during the day, then you would know that during a typical day, you would be best to leave or over estimate the time you schedule for your tasks to allow for this. It's like trying to put two pints into a one pint glass, if you know it's not going to fit, then don't try and do it.

Batch tasks together

In your daily activity plan put groups of similar work together so that you can achieve most effectiveness and productivity. Typical activities that can be easily batched, are, for instance, outgoing telephone calls.

A list of calls with telephone numbers along each side can be generated. These should be time scheduled in order that you can make one call after another in a fairly intensive fashion. Apply

Make sure you have everything you need before you start a task. *Proper Planning Prevents Pitifully Poor Performance.*

the same methodology in producing letters, working on the computer, visiting colleagues around the office, filing and so on.

In many cases we find that people suffer from the Butterfly Syndrome – 'flitting' from one task to another, perhaps in an almost random fashion during the day. They may start by opening the post, the post will then divert them to going and seeing a couple of people in their team to delegate pieces of work. On returning to their desk, they make a couple of calls, then remembering a letter or memo they haven't written from yesterday, they begin that. On almost completing this, they notice some other piece of paperwork which needs attention, and divert to this. Later they will perhaps return to completing their letter/memo, but probably not before being distracted by more phone calls, visits around the office and ad hoc paperwork.

Every time you stop or start a task, it takes a small element of time. Simply picking the paper, loading the file, finding the number for the person to telephone and just mentally changing tasks can take two or three minutes at the end of each task. If you do this ten or fifteen times during the day, which is not uncommon, this can lead to a full hour of wasted unproductive time.

Plan your week in advance

Whether you choose to use a week to view calendar or time planner for this or simply create a weekly planner on paper or perhaps a computer programme, the effect is the same. It will allow you to be able to schedule and 'make' time for things which are important but not yet urgent. In this way things can be more carefully scheduled.

The advantages of creating a weekly plan first thing on a Monday or last thing on a Sunday or Friday night are as follows:

1. It gives you a sense of proportion for the work which is most important.
2. By writing the plan down it actually helps you make more of a commitment by being more disciplined to do the things that you should do.

Select the prime time that you operate best. Some of us are morning people, some afternoon; plan for your best time so that you get your high yield jobs done then.

3. When you are wondering what to do next you can look at your plan for guidance. *If you find yourself completing tasks quicker or sooner than you anticipated, simply bring other tasks across from your scratch pad or To-do list.*
4. Having a weekly plan is also a great asset in trying to deflect distractions and interruptions. By showing people your weekly plan when you are trying to say that you are busy, actually looks very convincing.
5. It gives you a sense of control. One of the most important elements of beginning to get more control is to *create* a sense of control in what you do. Sitting down and taking a few moments to make a weekly plan will certainly help you do that.

Applying the 80/20 rule

Vilfredo Pareto (1848-1923) was an Italian economist and political sociologist who devised the 80:20 rule – the law of the trivial many and the critical few. This rule says that, in many business activities, 80 per cent of the potential value can be achieved from just 20 per cent of the effort, and that one can spend the remaining 80 per cent of effort for relatively little return.

Pareto's Law is about concentrating on what's important. Stated simply: the significant items in any group normally account for a relatively small proportion of the total. For example, 80 per cent of your sales probably come from 20 per cent of your customers. So concentrating most energy on this 20 per cent will bring you the best results.

Insurance companies put this into practice: 80 per cent of car accidents are caused by 20 per cent of drivers, so they charge these people much more to cover the higher risks involved.

Applying the rule

How does the rule apply to your customer? It is almost certain that your profitability depends mainly on your ability to satisfy just 20 per cent of them. You can't, of course, forget the other

80 per cent completely. But you would need more than a 24-hour day to put equal emphasis on their demands. The 80/20 rule can be used to identify new business prospects. Analysing the top 20 per cent of your customers should enable you to determine which businesses, or types of business, you need to target to win the best quality new clients.

Improve cash flow

On the accounts side, 80 per cent of the money you are owed will probably be due from only 20 per cent of your customers. In this instance, it is critical to chase large outstanding bills first, rather than going methodically through customer invoices from A to Z, irrespective of the amount owed.

One 80/20 technique is to put annual pound value on the decision. For example, a decision that can save you £100, but which will recur once a week (£5,200 annual savings) is far more important than a decision on £1,000 in an isolated situation that will not recur.

Manage your time

You can apply Pareto's Law in your work place where hundreds of things need your attention! Some things are very important, some less so, and others are worthless. Part of making the law work for you is learning how to prioritise and how much time to allocate to each task. It is distinguishing between urgent and important tasks. Being urgent does not make something important. And urgent jobs don't always have the highest pay off. They are often unplanned and generally get priority over important jobs. If you're honest, you'll probably find you spend 80 per cent of your time achieving 20 per cent of your goal – leaving just 20 per cent of your time to achieve 80 per cent of your goal. This is madness and obviously makes bad business sense.

So can you find a way to deal with the time-consuming but non-revenue generating aspects in less time? Like delegating?

Once you're skilled in this technique, you will find yourself spending more time on the important things. It's not easy and you may have to do some careful planning initially. But once the processes and mechanisms are in place, you'll end up being able to concentrate on the vital parts of the business.

Pareto analysis

What is it ?

Pareto Analysis is a simple method for separating the major causes (the 'vital few') of a problem, from the minor ones ('trivial many').

Why use it ?

Pareto Analysis can help you prioritise and focus resources where they are most needed. It can also help you measure the impact of an improvement by comparing before and after. When giving presentations, Pareto diagrams are a visually effective means of displaying the relative importance of causes, problems or other conditions.

Constructing a Pareto diagram

1. Assemble the data to be analysed. You may need to design a checksheet to collect it.
2. Add up the total of each item under analysis.
3. List the items in order of magnitude, starting with the largest.
4. Calculate.

   Work out the total of all the items, and the percentage that each item represents of the total. Beside each item write the cumulative total and cumulative percentage.
5. Draw a bar chart.

   Use the y-axis (vertical) to show the volume of what you are comparing (frequency, cost, time etc); list the items from left to right in the x-axis (horizontal), arranged according to size, with the largest on the left. If there are a lot of items, you may group together those containing the fewest number into an 'Other' category placed on the far right as the last bar.

Above each item draw a bar to a height that matches its frequency or count on the y-axis. The bars should all be the same width and not have gaps between them. Under the horizontal axis label each of these bars.

6. Draw in the cumulative curve.
   To do this, draw a line from where the axes start to the upper right-hand corner of the first bar. Place a dot here and next to it write the percentage calculated for that item. Make a second dot directly above the top right hand corner of the second bar to represent the cumulative total (ie the total of the first and second item added together). Join it to the first dot and write the cumulative percentage beside it. Continue until the last cumulative total has been plotted. On the right-hand side of the diagram, next to the last bar, draw in a second vertical axis which starts at zero and has 100 per cent aligned with the end of the cumulative curve.
7. Label the diagram with a title and any other necessary items; the date it was drawn, the source of the data, etc.
8. Interpret the diagram.

In general, the items requiring priority action, the 'vital few', will appear on the left of the diagram where the slope of the curve is steepest. When comparing before and after, if the improvement measures are effective either the order of the bars will change or the curve will be much flatter.

Sometimes it is helpful to do more than one Pareto diagram, based on different units of measurement eg the type of error which occurs most frequently may be the cheapest to correct; in this case it would be appropriate to do a Pareto diagram based on cost to see which error accounts for most of the correction cost.

Setting priorities

Urgent v important

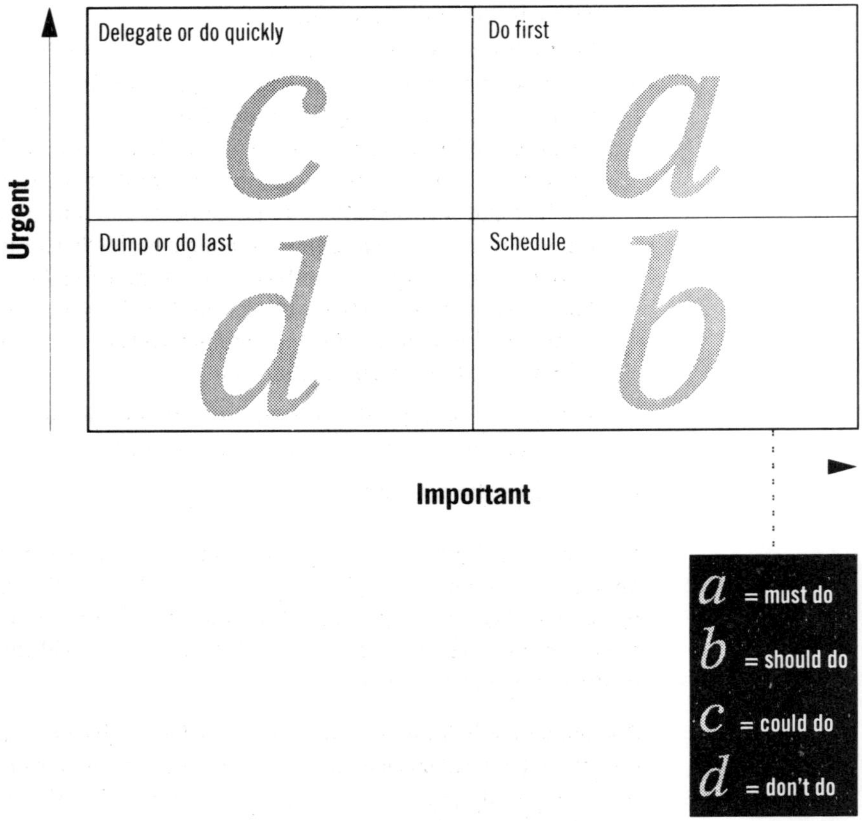

Figure 4: Using a priority matrix

In trying to decide what to do first, and which is the greatest priority, a priority matrix can be very useful. It looks at all the tasks and activities and To-dos that we may have to do and assesses each on two simple criteria, how urgent, and how important it is. Whilst the importance rating is obviously subjective and is of relative importance from one task to another, the urgency factor can perhaps be slightly more precise with dates, times and so on being established.

If you are given work to do, then one piece of information we need to know when people delegate things to us is what do they mean by urgent. We need to be alert to such phrases as 'this is really urgent' or 'this is very urgent' and also when people say 'I would like this as soon as possible.' They may well have some form of expectation or requirement, and by finding out when is the ideal time, or the latest time they need to have it completed by, we can be better able to schedule the work into our working day.

The importance scale can also be related directly to our main job purpose or objectives or the monthly, quarterly objectives we were working on at that time relating each task or activity to whatever helps us achieve these objectives better.

The advantage of using the matrix is that once you know where an activity sits in either box one, two, three or four, you can have a much clearer idea of where to schedule it in your day and when and where it should be done.

Outlined below are some examples of the type of work that might be found in each box of the priority matrix (refer to page 56). You will also see some simple instructions that we need to give to ourselves.

Box A

Anything in Box A is a *must do* activity or task. These are both urgent and important and we should either do them first or do them now.

Box B

These activities are important but not urgent, at least not yet. These activities need to be scheduled and these are typically *should do* activities. They need to be the things we work on after we finish our Box A.

Box C

Box C activities are those things which are urgent but not relatively speaking that important. We may be doing quite a few of these already, we need to make time so that we can concentrate on Box B. Therefore tasks in Box C need to be done quickly or delegated, or maybe consider not even doing them. Remember, just because something is urgent it does not mean to say that it's important.

Box D

Box D are categories that are relatively not that important and not very urgent. If we find ourselves working on these activities, perhaps unconsciously being distracted by them, then the reason is probably because we enjoy them therefore they are more fun or it's simply a habit or routine we have got in to.

In moving forward from here to plan your time and make best use of your week and day, the strategy you need to develop is to minimise the amount of time you spend in activities C and D, and increase the amount of time you spend doing things in Box B. In the short-term this may seem a difficult challenge. You may well have a great many things already in Box A. This is typically what people mean by the term Crisis Management. However, by beginning the shift to putting things into Box B you can tackle things which are important before they become urgent, and, in some cases, perhaps prevent activities happening in Box A through better planning, preparation and prevention activities.

For example, if you received a memo for a Performance Appraisal, that was scheduled for a month's time, you would probably turn to that day and schedule it in your diary. Typically most people would then complete the form later. This may often be forgotten or certainly shuffled around the desk for the next few weeks until the day before the appraisal when you suddenly remember that you haven't completed your form. It now becomes a Box A activity – both important and urgent – and time has to be found in the day, perhaps after hours, to make time for this activity. Simply recognising that preparing a Performance Appraisal is an important activity, means it can be scheduled in advance before it becomes urgent. This will help us to make the time to do this and encourage us to have the self-discipline to complete it.

The night before list

Many people find that one of the reasons that they don't make written To-do lists in the morning, is because that by the time they sit down or get into their office they are already too busy. If this is the case, you may want to try an alternative method.

Before leaving the night before take a piece of paper or your notebook and write down six tasks in order of priority that you want to do the next day. It is important to limit yourself to only six and to schedule them by priority.

This way when you come back in the next morning, you will find on your desk a short prioritised list to begin work on.

Consider moving closer to your place of work. This is a big step, but if you saved 15 minutes of commuting time each day, you would gain an additional three weeks of working (or playing) time per year!

The sixty-four thousand dollar question

The term 'sixty-four thousand dollar question,' whilst attributable to a popular game show, actually comes from the memoirs of Andrew Carnegie, one of the most successful entrepreneurs and businessmen of the early part of this century in America.

He is reported to have employed a consultant to answer the question, 'How can I become more successful?' The consultant took on the assignment, charging Carnegie a reported $64,000 for the answer. This was a huge amount of money at the time, and is not inconsiderable now. After two weeks of following Carnegie around, sitting in meetings, travelling with him, seeing how he made decisions and so on, the consultant simply repeated the expression – **ONLY DO THE MOST IMPORTANT THINGS** – that is the key to how you can become more successful. In his memoirs, Carnegie said that it was the best piece

Display a sign or poster: 'Only do the most important things'

of advice that he ever paid for and it was worth many times more than what he actually paid.

When you go about your daily work activity and routine, the one question you need to keep asking yourself is – am I working on the most important things right now? If you can answer that question and say 'yes', then the results and the productivity and benefits will come towards you. If the answer is 'no' or 'not really', then stop what you are doing and move onto something that is more important for you at that time.

First things first

DO FIRST THINGS FIRST AND SECOND THINGS LAST OR NOT AT ALL.

If you have a very reactive job or your time is particularly precious, you will find it advantageous to develop the habit of doing first things first. This means doing the highest priority (Box A) at the beginning of each and every day, hour or week.

Avoid tasks that are easy or you enjoy for just those reasons. Keep these to last and use them as personal rewards.

Knowing that these have been completed you can then perhaps allow some of the crisis management, fire fighting and ad hoc activities that come along to take your time, knowing that you have taken care of the most important activities. There is an old saying – if you lose an hour in the morning you will take all day to find it – if you put off important tasks and replace them with reactive tasks then not only will you not find the time to do them, your results will suffer accordingly.

How to gain one hour a day – every day

Learn to know where your time goes

Expect the unexpected

Create a non-interruption zone (NIZ)

Dump trivia

Do less and achieve more – delegation

Anticipate and look for opportunity time

Speed up routine tasks: How to speed up these activities

Stop doing other people's work

Concentration of power

Clean up your communications: How to win friends and influence people

Learn to know where your time goes
Expect the unexpected
Create a non-interruption zone (NIZ)
Dump trivia
Do less and achieve more – delegation
Anticipate and look for opportunity time
Speed up routine tasks: How to speed up these activities
Stop doing other people's work
Concentration of power
Clean up your communications: How to win friends and influence people
Learn to know where your time goes
Expect the unexpected
Create a non-interruption zone (NIZ)
Dump trivia
Do less and achieve more – delegation
Anticipate and look for opportunity time
Speed up routine tasks: How to speed up these activities
Stop doing other people's work
Concentration of power
Clean up your

three

Learn to know where your time goes

What is more important – time or money?

Some people say that time is money, which in the business world is usually true, but unless you are absolutely flat broke the chances are that time is more important to you than money – because time is irreplaceable.

Whilst we may track our money, most of us never really analyse where we are spending our time. Indeed, experience shows that most people don't know where the day goes. You may often hear people saying, 'Is that the time already? I don't know where the afternoon has gone!' So, in order to have a better appreciation of where our time goes there is one simple rule we can use, it is called the Activity or Time Log.

Try to avoid being placed on hold on the telephone. It takes less time to call back.

An Activity Log

An Activity Log is a highly effective way of monitoring the way you spend your time. If you work purely from memory it is easy to believe that you spent all your day working, and consider that your use of time is good. If you keep an Activity Log for a few days you may be surprised to see precisely how much of your day is wasted. Without modifying your behaviour, note down the things you do as you do them, from the moment you come into the office. Every time you change activities, whether opening mail, working, making coffee, dealing with colleagues, gossiping etc, note down the time of the change.

As well as noting activities, it is worth noting how you feel, whether alert, flat, tired, energetic, etc. This should be done periodically throughout the day. Once you have logged your time for several days, analyse the log. You may be alarmed to see the length of time you spend opening mail, dealing with disruptions or doing low value jobs! You may also see that you are energetic in some parts of the day, and flat in other parts. This can depend on your rest breaks, the times and amounts you eat, and quality of your nutrition. The Activity Log gives you some basis for experimenting with these variables.

A Time Log

A Time Log is a simple form that once a month you carry around with you or leave by the side of your desk to track your actual time usage. Every 15 minutes tick the box for the category of activity that you have been working on for most of that time. Fill in your own activities on a form depending on your job description or job profile. Whilst it takes a degree of self-discipline to keep remembering to do the Time Log, so long as you keep it in a good place, perhaps taped to the front of the diary, it is quick and easy. Once you have done a Time Log you will recognise the benefits and be much more motivated to do it, at a time that is available to you. Once you have completed your Time Log you can ask the following key questions:

- Did I do anything that wasted my time?
- Did I work on things at the right time of the day?
- Did I put important things off until later?
- Am I guilty of the Butterfly Syndrome – jumping from one thing to another perhaps, without completing tasks?
- Did I do other people's work for them?
- Did I do anything that wasted the time of other people?
- Am I doing things that are not part of my main job description or moving towards my goals and objectives?

These questions will uncover new understandings on how you use your time now, which in turn can lead you to better appropriation of your time in the future. People that complete a Time Log can easily identify a time saving of at least an hour in any typical day. This can be done by simply stopping the time spent chatting, travelling or doing unnecessary tasks or even from speeding up certain routine tasks. We can also identify how much time we take dealing with interruptions or sitting in meetings. When added together, over days or weeks, this can be quite shocking. Do not be too critical by measuring every last minute. It is only the general training that we are looking for.

If you manage a team of people having them complete a Time Log can be a useful tool in understanding the most important part of their job and some of their time management challenges.

Expect the unexpected

Expect travel delays, so when travelling listen to cassette tapes on time management, self-motivation and similar subjects, as well as any that are available in your professional field.

Murphy's Law states that if anything can possibly go wrong, it probably will. You can save an hour a day by preventing, preparing, planning and looking for opportunities for Murphy to strike.

Here are some common examples:

1. Call ahead to double check appointments/meetings the day before travelling. The day you don't check will be the day that the appointment is cancelled or you have the time wrong.
2. Have things to do for when you arrive or travel.
3. Double check any complex itineraries, plans or projects. Make sure that there is a buffer if things go wrong and need to be recovered.
4. Sensitive or critical projects should be checked and double checked.
5. Always try and build a slight buffer into any promises that you might give, particularly for customers.
6. Allow time in your diary or schedule for things that do go wrong which may require your time and attention.
7. Learn to anticipate the unexpected.
8. Try to anticipate the time of the week or month when you will have the last minute jobs.
9. Develop check lists, process and clear standards of performance for critical outputs in your job or business.
10. Make sure people work to consistent methods allowing time to check and double check what they do. One missed point could create hours of work for somebody else.

Create a non-interruption zone (NIZ)

You can get more done in one hour of quiet concentration than you can in two with interruptions. However, create this during the day, not by staying late or getting in early.

If you want to make sure you have some clear space or time to do the most important tasks, then set up a daily time to have a NIZ. This is essential. A NIZ or non-interruption zone is usually a period of time, say an hour, when your staff and customers know that it is not a good time to disturb you. This leaves you to focus clearly, without interruption on the most important, high quality tasks.

The way you create a NIZ is simple: inform staff and train them that you prefer not to be interrupted at a certain time. Pick the same time each day or give a clear communication signal every day for about a week or two. After a while people will realise that that time is a standard NIZ and you will no longer have to mention it.

Don't be deceived by the simplicity of this idea. People who have tried this would testify that one hour of uninterrupted time is probably worth one or two of normal time. You can get so much more done and usually the quality of the work is so much greater.

Dump trivia

One of the things that you need to tackle is the need to stop doing unimportant tasks – what we call trivia tasks. These are things that no longer need to be done and do not contribute anything to your effectiveness, results or product ability.

We may tackle them first because they are short and simple, but if there is no real importance or urgencies to them, then we should not be doing them at all. You may find that you can ease your conscience by delegating some of the daily trivial tasks that consume your day. You may also find that you can do wonders by speeding up your work load and how you tackle it. Simply opening the mail or doing other things such as filing with a stop-watch ticking can actually concentrate you to work faster and quicker to get thing done. One suggestion is not to do them at all:

Less is more; do less and achieve more!

- Can you survive without them?
- Will they impact on your effectiveness?
- Will anyone notice the difference if you do them or not?

If the answer to each of these is 'no', then let go of these tasks.

Do less and achieve more – delegation

LEARN TO DELEGATE URGENT BUT NOT RELEVANTLY IMPORTANT TASKS.

Another habit that we need to break is the tendency to try and do everything ourselves. Many people who are promoted tend to take tasks with them from their previous job.

For example, a sales person promoted to team leader may try to hold on to some of their accounts. They may also try to keep doing the things that they have always done, such as their own expense forms, letters and so on. If something is not particularly important, and the other people around you can be trained to do it, then the time saving can be considerable.

As some things might be urgent, it is important to be able to delegate and have it done quickly by people who are competent and who have the time to do it. For instance, can you train people to respond and return calls from customers or particular types of colleagues? Can filing and paperwork be handled as it happens rather than stored up? Even if you work in a small business or non-commercial environment there are still many tasks that you can delegate – sometimes to an external organisation, maybe to a typing bureau, a photocopying or graphic design company. All this means letting go of the trivial and less important things and focusing on what you need for your team tasks, goals and performance criteria.

Most of the top business executives recognise the limitations of what they can do themselves. They know that to accomplish great goals, you have to build and depend on those who work under you. As they grow and become successful, largely through delegation, the manager accomplishes the larger goals for the company.

Success is a joint partnership venture in delegation.

Poor excuses for not delegating

'I can do this work better than anyone else.'

'If I delegate to others, what will I do?'

'This job is so important that I am the only one who can do it.'

There are probably a lot of reasons not to delegate, but few good ones. Almost by definition, if we are to succeed and grow and if our people are to succeed and grow, we must continually delegate effectively!

Many people have tried delegation once and concluded it was more trouble that it was worth. Delegation is a skill that has to be learned and then practised. Mistakes will be made and it will be slow at first, but in the long run is the only important factor. When you delegate effectively, your people grow, morale improves, efficiency improves, more of the desired results get achieved. The benefits of delegation far outweigh the difficulties.

Who is to blame?

For effective delegation to take place, the delegate must have a full understanding of the results to be achieved. It is even better if the 'doer' can work out the details of how to do a task, in their own way. After all, if the end results are what you expect and limits and boundaries are not exceeded, why shouldn't the person do it their way?

They should! It gets people involved in the delegated work. They need to feel the job is more theirs than yours... otherwise, they are just robots carrying out your instructions.

If you don't have the necessary people to delegate to – outsource or use temporary staff. If delegating is the best, or perhaps the only way of getting something done on time, it might be worth paying for.

Delegating to others is difficult for most of us and hard for the other person at first. That is why it is so important to follow-up and when they have done a successful job (even if it was not as good as we could have done), we must be quick to praise and thank the person.

It is true of many people that given greater challenges, they will accomplish more. A person who knows that they are growing, learning new things, acquiring new skills and earning more money, is a happy person. This is one of the major keys to developing and keeping good people. Delegation plays a key role in this positive attitude. You are the coach and cheerleader. You coach them to be successful, then cheer when they succeed. This is the attitude of the manager who is a successful delegator. It is up to you to build people and make them successful. Delegation is a central principle in achieving these goals for the people you supervise.

Anticipate and look for opportunity time

There will be times in the day when you have time on your hands. This can be very frustrating if you do not have enough time to spend in the office. You may be in a traffic jam, in an airport, waiting for an appointment or meeting and you are sitting there waiting, watching the clock. This is *opportunity time.* Spare time which you didn't necessarily know was going to happen, although we could probably anticipate having. It is important to have things with you to work on, such as:

- *The reading file.* Open your post or mail into your brief-case. The important but non-urgent memos, letters, magazines and so on can then be reviewed later when you have this opportunity time.
- *Planning and goal setting.* Have a notebook and pen to hand. You can sit down quietly, perhaps without interruption, because of where you are and make notes clearly about some plans, goals and objectives. Every time you rewrite a goal you re-affirm to yourself your direction and its importance.

- Carry with you letters that you would like to read.
- Carry a tape recorder or dictating machine.
- Keep a mobile phone or have a charge card call facility available. If you have a few minutes simply grab your Action Plan and To-do list or work your way through a number of telephone calls.

Speed up routine tasks

Much of what you do may be fairly routine, such as travelling, filing, standard meetings, editing, making and receiving telephone calls, working on the computer and so on. By just being more organised, many people have found they can save three 30/40 minute periods per day.

How to speed up these activities

1. Use a timer. Set it for say ten minutes and try and complete the task before the alarm goes off.
2. Put a clock in front of you and keep looking at it as you work as quickly as possible.
3. Make calls and do standard tasks where possible standing up. This may help you concentrate and be quicker and shorter in execution.
4. Promise yourself a reward when you finish your activities, such as a cup of coffee.
5. Fit the activities in and buffer them up against key meetings, lunch breaks and so on so that they have an end point that they cannot go beyond. This may help you to concentrate them into a fixed piece of time.
6. Work with a sense of energy and urgency. Launch into the task and don't stop until you have completed it.
7. Do one thing at a time and don't stop until it's finished.

Stop doing other people's work

If you are looking to save an hour a day you might find that 60 minutes can be found in tasks you do that other people should be doing for themselves. Whilst it is nice to help people and we should be as accommodating as possible, we have to strike a balance between protecting our own time, goals and ambitions and helping others achieve theirs. It does not mean saying 'no' all the time. It just means looking very objectively at the tasks that people are asking for help with. Is it something they should be doing or could be doing?

If this is the case, do one or two things:

1. Politely say '**no**' explaining that you cannot deal with that as you thought it should be them doing it and not you.
2. Redirect them to somebody else who you think is more appropriate to help them.
3. Explain to them how to do it, giving them the confidence to go away and try it. (The reason they may be asking you is because they do not feel competent or confident themselves to complete the activity well enough.)
4. Say you will do the task but then don't complete it, this is particularly useful if you feel it impossible to say '**no**'. Whilst it may be embarrassing and uncomfortable when they come back and find the task or activity not completed, the chances are they will not ask you again, as you have let them down once. When they do come back make sure you explain why and apologise!

Concentration of power

WORK FROM AN ACTION PLAN AND DO ONE THING AT A TIME

An Action Plan is a brief list of tasks that you have to carry out to achieve an objective. It differs from a To-do list in that it focuses on the *achievement* of a goal, rather than focusing on goals to be achieved in a period of time. Wherever you want to achieve something, drawing up an Action Plan allows you to concentrate on the stages of that achievement, and monitor your progress towards that achievement.

Clean up your communications

1. Think first, talk second

When dealing with an issue involving another person, first become aware of your thoughts, feelings and any intuitive insights you might have around the issue. What do you want to convey to him or her? What **do** you want?

2. Timing

Out of fairness and respect, choose a mutually convenient time and place to discuss one issue only. Agree on which issue will be discussed, and on the length of your session.

3. Relaxed environment

Beforehand, prepare and calm yourself. Do your favourite relaxation technique, or simply take 3-4 very deep breaths and let them out with a sigh. Perhaps do some stretches or some kind of movement to relax your body.

4. Relax your body language

- Maintain relaxed eye contact. Remember to blink and breathe! Check in often to see whether you're relaxed or tense. Tensing, then letting go of your neck and shoulder muscles helps.
- Make large circles with your shoulders forward and back. Raise and alternately knit your eyebrows then let go to relieve scalp and forehead tightness.
- Open and close your mouth to help jaw tension. Use whatever works for you! Maybe you need to change where or how you're sitting. To make whatever adjustments might be necessary, take time out and agree on when to start again.

5. Get in touch with what you are thinking and feeling

This is done by first filtering out external 'noise', especially interruptions, telephone calls, television, etc. Next, before your meeting sit quietly and think in detail about an issue or person. During a conversation, dampen down your internal thoughts and focus only on that moment, become aware of any instinctive sensations that you experience as one or other of you are talking.

6. Become clear of your intentions. What do you WANT?

Most mis-communication involves a lack of clarity, deliberate or otherwise – about what you or a colleague are aiming to achieve. Stating this clearly and early can greatly help communication and rapport. Even if the different outcomes are stated, this can then speed-up finding solutions. ·

7. Voice tone

- With a pleasant tone of voice (no whining!), use 'I' statements. This takes it out of the blaming, judging arena. Ask yourself a few questions: 'Do I want to fight?' 'Am I insisting on being right, no matter what?' Or, 'Would I rather create an atmosphere of mutual trust, safety and understanding?' Am I coming from a place of love or fear?'
- If you are feeling angry or over-reactive, let the other person know and reschedule your time together. Then breathe deeply, take a walk, or whatever it takes to get you calmed down and rational.

8. Restating

Then, ask the other person to repeat back what you have just said. They may have incorrectly heard and/or misinterpreted your communication. This crucial step will give you more clarity and understanding around the issue.

9. Active listening

Now, it's the other person's turn. Listen openly, attentively and compassionately. Take a few deep breaths. Then, paraphrase what they said.

10. Brainstorming

Brainstorm for solutions. Open up to creative ideas that may not occur to you normally. Be willing to compromise. Agree on at least one step you can take to immediately resolve or at least relieve the tensions around the issue.

Do not be discouraged if the resolution is incomplete at this time. Reschedule to come back to the issue again, if necessary. Commit to take as long as it takes to be resolved or at least relieved. At the end of your 'session' you will feel empowered knowing you have taken vital steps toward having what you want.

How to win friends and influence people

How to Win Friends and Influence People is a book by Dale Carnegie. Good time management, influence and motivation go hand in hand. The chapters in the book are listed below. For more insights, read (or re-read the book).

1. Don't criticise, condemn or complain
2. Give honest, sincere appreciation
3. Arouse in the other person an eager want
4. Become genuinely interested in other people
5. Smile
6. Remember that a person's name is to that person the sweetest and most important sound
7. Be a good listener
8. Talk in terms of the other person's interest
9. Make the other person feel important and do it sincerely
10. The only way to get the best of an argument is to avoid it
11. Show respect for the other person's opinion and never say, 'you're wrong'
12. If you are wrong, admit it quickly and emphatically
13. Begin in a friendly way
14. Get the other person saying 'yes, yes' immediately

15. Let the other person do a great deal of the talking
16. Let the other person feel that the idea is his or hers
17. Try honestly to see things from the other person's point of view
18. Be sympathetic with the other person's ideas and desires
19. Appeal to the nobler motives
20. Dramatise your ideas
21. Throw down a challenge

Positive goal setting

The importance of goal setting

Understanding how goals work: Why don't more people set goals?

Setting S.M.A.R.T goals

How to set goals: What? • Why? • When? • How?

Review goals regularly: Using creative visualisation • How goals help you to get more done

An introduction to goal setting: Why set goals? • Setting well-formed outcomes

Seven steps to goal achievement

Steps to your goals: Overview • Is having a goal enough? • Strategies for personal growth

Using behaviour modification principles: Define your goal • What is involved? • Where are you starting from? • Reassess your goals • Know how • Choose your reinforcers • Record your progress • Analyse your progress and make improvements • Reward your successes

Create more balance in your life

Self-recording as a tool for self-development: Behavioural contracting

The importance of goal setting

Understanding how goals work: Why don't more people set goals?

Setting S.M.A.R.T goals

How to set goals: What? • Why? When? • How?

Review goals regularly: Using creative visualisation • How goals help you to get more done

An introduction to goal setting: Why set goals? • Setting well-formed outcomes

Seven steps to goal achievement

Steps to your goals: Overview • Is having a goal enough? • Strategies for personal growth

Using behaviour modification principles: Define your goal • What is involved? • Where are you starting

four

The importance of goal setting

A study that was begun at Harvard University in 1953 dramatically highlights the importance of setting clear and defined goals in helping achieve and maximise potential. The study asks a group of graduates as they left the university how many of them had clear written well-defined goals for their careers and lives following on from their university education. The study tracked these individuals over the course of the next 20 years. In 1973 they found a very interesting statistic. In 1953 only five per cent of the graduates admitted to having clear goals for their careers and lives, by 1973 those five per cent were worth more in financial terms and exceeded in other areas as well than the other 95 per cent put together. Whilst this is a fairly astonishing statistic, it is not uncommon when you look at the distinctions between the people or groups of individuals that set clear defined goals and those who don't.

We can find examples of the above not only in business or in financial achievement, but also in education, sports, theatre and the arts.

The importance of goal setting is very difficult to overstate. What is it that knits a team together? Typically it is a common objective or goal. What is it that motivates people to achieve higher and higher levels of success, when they have probably already exceeded not only their own goals but also the achievements of many other people? It is their desire and ambition to achieve higher and higher goals. What is it that makes people work harder, try more inventive ideas and stretch themselves? Working consistently towards a worthwhile or important goal.

Understanding how goals work

Why don't more people set goals?

Rewrite and re-prioritise your goals and activities at least every three months. The world changes, we change and so we must review our goals.

There may be several answers to this question. The first and perhaps the most common is that people are not aware of the power for setting goals. Once you are aware of the goal setting power, then you can begin to use the methods and techniques of goal setting. Over and over again you can draw into your life and work results and achievements far beyond your imagination. The way to do this is to simply begin to set small practical and achievable goals.

Show that the system works and then move forward to more ambitious and challenging objectives. For example, try this exercise, set yourself a simple, perhaps work related, goal that you would like to achieve in the next 30 days. Make it something that you would not normally do but make sure it is within your capabilities. Put it through the ideas in this chapter and see how easily and quickly it comes into reality and also how motivating and satisfying it is to know that you have achieved it.

Another reason why people don't like to set goals is the fear of failure or embarrassment if the goals don't work out. Do not share your goals with people, that way you can't be criticised for not achieving them. I think that there is nothing wrong with setting a goal and maybe not achieving it as easily or as quickly or in the way that you expected. The real mistake is not setting goals in the first place for things that you would like to do.

Setting S.M.A.R.T goals

In order for goal setting to work effectively, a goal or objective or outcome needs to meet certain simple criteria. *A goal should be Specific, Measurable, Achievable, Realistic and Time bounded.*

To be *specific* a goal should have a clearly defined outcome. You should be able to describe how you will know when you have achieved a goal. A goal should be stated in positive terms. Instead of thinking of what you don't want, focus on what you do want. For example, instead of thinking of being a non-smoker, focus instead on being fit and healthy.

Your goal should be *measurable*, it should be clearly defined to let you know how you are doing and, of course, when you get there.

Achievable is a more subjective statement. How achievable do you feel the goal is? This question can make you realise how much work and effort is needed to achieve the goal. The most important thing that you need to do is to focus on the activities that you need to do to achieve the goal. If you can create an activity plan for the goal, then the goal is probably achievable, that is, if you are prepared to do the necessary work. How realistic is the goal? For example, you might set yourself a goal of achieving a certain promotion in your work by a certain date.

Alternatively, you might set yourself a goal of spending more time with the family and getting promoted. Might these two goals be in conflict? So which of the goals is more realistic now? It could be realistic to get promotion without putting in hours and hours of work. If you follow the advice in this book it certainly is.

Finally, the goal should have a *time scale*, a goal without a deadline is an exercise in self deletion. So make sure that you put some realistic deadlines and time scales to your goal. These may need to be adjusted as you move forward, but make sure that you adjust them for a good reason only and see if you can use a deadline to focus your attention, energy and commitment to get the goal finished.

How to set goals

Setting a goal, whatever it is, business or personal, long-term or short-term, simple or complex, is a very easy process. There are four headings that you need to use to create a goal plan. Below are four questions which need to be completed in order for the goal to begin to take shape. It is important to do this in writing, on paper. This alerts a sub-conscious mind, a part of the mind that we understand gives us the motivation, desire and determination to see the goal through.

What?

Write a statement of what the goal is; make the goal sound compelling. Write it down perhaps as if you have already achieved it.

Why?

Why do you want the goal? Write down your reasons. Why is the goal important to you? What will you gain by achieving the goal? How will you feel when you have got there or how will you feel if you don't achieve the goal? What is the alternative? Create as many good sound reasons as you can. Whilst goal setting is straightforward it is not always easy. Along the way you are going to hit obstacles and problems. The reason why you want the goal, and the feelings that you will get on completion, will help you push through the difficulties and come out the other side as a goal achiever.

When?

When do you want the goal? Create a start date and a finish date. Write them down clearly.

How?

Action Plan. The goal needs to be broken down into clearly defined and personal stated action. Make sure that the goal doesn't have too many actions which rely on other people. This can take the power away from you being able to achieve the goal yourself. Clearly this may not always be possible but it is important to have your own personal action plan on how the goal can be achieved. For example, if you set yourself a goal of running a marathon you could write yourself a training schedule.

Review goals regularly

Goals are not something that you simply set and then forget about. Goal setting should be considered as a map on a journey. If you are travelling across an area you are unfamiliar with, you would regularly refer to a map looking at the landmarks, the signs, the compass, whatever, all the time checking your progress to see where you are up to and where you need to go next.

The same is true of goal setting, take time out regularly – maybe on a daily, weekly or possibly monthly basis – to write and review your goals for both personal and work situations. Focus on a few simple goals, perhaps two or three key goals in each area, maybe also set two or three medium to long-term goals in each of the areas, perhaps personal, family and career goals.

Try looking five and ten years on, where would you like to be in ten years time?

- What sort of person will you be?
- What would your hobbies and sports activities be?
- How would your friends describe you as an individual?

These can all alert you to the goals that you may have for the distant future. Set these goals and work backwards, build them into your daily and weekly routines making sure that every day you are moving in some way closer to the goals and achievements and objectives that you would like to have in the future.

Using creative visualisation

A lot of work has been done into how we can best use the technique of goal setting to motivate and bring ourselves closer to what we desire.

Creative visualisation, known to ancient sages and religious mystics for centuries, and now more recently adopted by Olympic athletes, has been proven to be effective and successful in creating compelling futures. In many ways we live in a world full of dreams come true, the thoughts, ideas, goals and concepts that people dream up and think in their heads end up being brought into reality by the process of working on them as clearly defined goals and outcomes.

On a regular basis, take time to simply relax, perhaps just as you go to sleep visualise your goal as clearly and as vividly in pictures as you possibly can. Maybe run a movie on a cinema screen, play it backwards and forwards, make it big, bright and vivid, show it in slow motion or close up, see yourself performing the goal, and achieving the goal in perfect style, achieving excellence in your mind's eye. Do this regularly and over time you will be able to develop the confidence and awareness and be able to see yourself in reality doing the things you vividly imagined.

How goals help you get more done

The value of goals in helping us achieve more and manage ourselves better on a daily basis is very simple. A goal will presumably be set about something that is important to us, either in our work or for us as individuals.

Therefore these goals are extrapolated out into our daily action plans. For example, if you had two or three key monthly goals and objectives which you either set, or set jointly with your manager for one particular month, your daily and weekly schedule could then be set to reflect your achievement and progress through the activities needed to bring those goals and objectives into being. For example, if one of the objectives had been to plan and run an exhibition for a new product launch, then that will focus your mind onto the key activities needed to make that happen. Choosing a venue, suppliers, designing brochures and so on, this can be simply planned when moving towards the goal and other activities and actions simply judged against it.

Take the time to review your goals on a daily basis, particularly as you write and re-write your Action Plans and To-do lists. Make sure you can answer the question, is what I am working on right now moving me towards one of my major goals? If it isn't, the tasks may well carry a no or nil satisfaction rating and you will feel frustrated and make little progress.

An introduction to goal setting

Success begins with the end in mind. It starts with deciding what you are trying to achieve – for example, the results that you are employed to deliver.

Why set goals?

There are two main reasons why it is so important to set clear, specific and realistic goals:

1. **You can't hit a target you can't see.**
2. **Goals, or clearly defined outcomes, are the keys to self-motivation.**

Goal setting is both a process and an attitude. Instead of basing what is possible on what you have been able to achieve in the past, you concentrate on what is achievable in the future. It allows you to expand your horizons on the plains of possibility and spot opportunities where others see nothing.

Write your main goals or objectives on 3" x 5" cards so that they can be carried and read regularly.

A goal is a dream taken seriously

Goal setting gives you direction, energy and commitment, and most importantly a way of taking some influence over your results. Whilst goals do not guarantee results, they allow you to set priorities, and to plan your work, time and your life more effectively, and with greater satisfaction. You need both 'results' goals and 'performance' goals. You also need to balance goals: between work, family and self-development.

Balanced goals

As well as setting specific goals for your sales and business ideals, you can also set goals for each area of your life. Try setting some goals for the following areas of your life. Some can be long-term goals, say two-three years, others short-term about two-three months, aim for about four-five of each type.

a. Personal and family goals
   - these are the reasons *why*

b. Business and career goals
   - these are the *what* goals

c. Self-development goals
   - these are the *how* goals

The secret of success and achievement is not just to become great in any area or task, but to maintain a sense of balance and proportion throughout all areas of your life.

Setting well-formed outcomes

Positive

- Think of what you want, rather than what you don't want.
- Ask: What would I really want?
- What would I rather have?

Own part

- Think of what you can actively do that is within your control.
- Ask: What will I be doing to achieve my outcome?
- How can I start and maintain it?

Specific

- Detail the outcome as specifically as possible.
- Ask: Who, where, when, what, how specifically?

Evidence

- Think of the sensory based evidence that will let you know you have got what you want.
- Ask: What will I see, hear and feel when I have it?
- How will I know when I have it?

Resources and choices

- Do you have adequate personal resources and choices?
- Ask: What resources or choices do I need to get the outcome?

Size

- Is the outcome the right size?
- If the outcome is too big, ask: What prevents me from getting this?
- If too small, ask: If I got this what would it do for me?

Value check

- Check for consequences in your life and relationships.
- Ask: Who else does it effect?
- How important is this to me really?
- Is it what I really want?
- Is it nice to have/achieve or need to achieve?
- What would happen if I got it? What would happen if I didn't?
- If I could have it straight away, would I take it? (congruity check)

Seven steps to goal achievement

Here is a seven step planning process to clarify and help you develop almost any goal – personal or organisational.

1. Realistic written goals

You must make your goals and objectives believable and achievable. Goals should have a 50/50 chance of success. Each goal must be aimed at the next logical step on the road to accomplishment.

When you write it down, you make it concrete. When you don't write it down you avoid making a commitment. Rules for written goals are:

1. be positive
2. be clear and specific
3. use vivid language.

If your goal is large – focus only on the first, smaller, steps.

2. **Why do you want what you want? How do you know when you've made it?**

   These are vital questions. The response are your reasons 'why'. List your reasons for each of your goals. Also, take a moment to analyse your starting point. Where are you starting from? Be specific.

Work out a Plan A and Plan B. What will you do if Plan A doesn't work out exactly as you hope?

3. **Identify the 'HOW'**

   Take time to consider the 'how' that will lead you to the 'what', especially considering:

   1. Knowledge
   2. People
   3. Skills

4. **Make a plan**

   A plan is a list of activities which is organised by priorities. Time spent in planning usually reaps big dividends in effectiveness.

5. **Identify the road-blocks**

   'Road-blocks' come to instruct, not to obstruct. List the obstacles that you can foresee and set priorities on these.

6. **Visualisation**

   Everything happens twice; once in the internal world, and then again in the external world.

One of the best times to visualise is last thing at night, just before going to sleep.

7. **Commitment**

   - How badly do you want what you want?
   - Are you really prepared to do whatever it takes and try until you succeed?
   - Success comes from actions, identify one thing that you can do right **NOW**, **TODAY** to start you on your course towards this goal.

Steps to your goals

Overview

In the mid 1950s, two psychologists Carl Rogers and Abraham Maslow rejected what they saw as the dehumanising negativism of psychology of the day. It promoted the idea that humans were not the masters of their destiny and that all their actions were governed by either unconscious processes dominated by primitive sexual urges (Sigmund Freud) or by the environment. They argued that both schools of thought failed to recognise the unique qualities of human behaviour: love, self-esteem, belonging, self-expression and creativity. It was exactly these unique qualities, they argued, which enabled people to make independent choices which gave them full control of their destiny.

Maslow's study of people who lead highly effective lives led him to conclude that we all have a hierarchy of needs that motivate us to action. The highest of these needs is our need to realise our true potential (self-realisation). To be the best we can – in the words of Maslow, 'what a man can be, he must be.'

According to Alfred Adler – doctor, ophthalmologist and psychiatrist – the foremost source of human motivation is a striving for superiority which he saw as 'a universal drive to adapt, improve oneself and master life's challenges.'

This need for self-realisation is so vital to us that if it is not satisfied, at least in part, it can lead to experiences of despair, despondency, boredom, apathy and alienation – a 'syndrome of decay.'

In an exhaustive study of 'burnout', Ayla Pines and her colleagues (Pines & Aronson, 1988; Pines, Aronson, & Kafry 1981) conclude that 'the cause of burnout (physical, emotional and mental exhaustion) lies in our need to believe that our lives are meaningful and that the things we do are useful, important even heroic.'

Abraham Maslow found that another important characteristic amongst highly effective people was that they all had clearly defined goals and a mission in life.

Is having a goal enough?

Clearly not, as anyone who has set himself or herself some goals soon realises. This is because the processes of achieving your goals invariably involves some sort of change in behaviour. This could be either eating less or eating more nutritious foods, exercising, working more effectively, spending more time studying, giving up habits such as smoking and drinking etc. More often it involves a whole reassessment of one's life, leading to a deeper understanding of oneself. Stephen Covey in *The Seven Habits of Highly Effective People*, emphasises this holistic approach to achieving success.

Another important reason why most people who set goals and then fail to achieve them is their ignorance of a process known as behaviour modification. The technology of behaviour modification has been applied with great success in various institutions which range from schools to prisons.

Strategies for personal growth

Take time to look at your current situation:

Three things that I do well or easily:

1. ______________________________

2. ______________________________

3. ______________________________

Three things that I do poorly or could easily improve upon:

1. ______________________________

2. ______________________________

3. ______________________________

Three talents that are not used at all or enough in what I do:

1. ______________________________

2. ______________________________

3. ______________________________

Three skills that I would like to develop or master and admire in others:

1. ______________________________

2. ______________________________

3. ______________________________

Three ideas for future self-development:

1. ______________________________

2. ______________________________

3. ______________________________

Using behaviour modification principles

Define your goal

Specify a goal or a set of goals that you want to achieve. Record these goals clearly and precisely. It is vitally important that at this stage you avoid thinking of reasons why you can't, rather than concentrate on how your life will change for the better if you could achieve these goals. Don't limit yourself, be as fanciful as you like. Later you will review and reassess your goals once you have more information about what is involved.

What is involved?

Identify the characteristics of success for the goals you specified. What has to be done? You could find this out by talking or reading about people who have achieved this goal or similar goals. Failing this you can use your imagination and visualise another person (not you) achieving this particular goal. What are the actions /activities that lead to success? It is important to take yourself out of the picture for the moment, because of our tendency to immediately focus on reasons why we can't.

The simplest way to assess what is involved is to think in terms of time. For instance, if your goal is to achieve top marks in your studies, estimate how many hours of study is required. If your goal is to achieve a certain level of income, how much time would there be to devote to activities which contribute to success.

Example of change

Sign your name here as you would normally do:

____

Now place the pen or pencil in the **opposite** hand to which you would normally use and sign your name again.

____

Apart from how difficult this might have been, consider how 'strange' and uncomfortable this seemed. You could easily learn to sign your name with either hand, usually far faster than you might think, however, the resistance to change may take longer to overcome.

Once you have a good idea of what it takes, or what you think it would take for someone else to achieve your specified goal, the next step is to find out what it would take for you to do the same thing. This is not as simple as it sounds since our perceptions about ourselves are likely to be very different from reality.

We need a baseline. A starting point. The only sure way to get an accurate baseline is to keep a record of the activities you identified for at least 21 days.

Where are you starting from?

Record a baseline. Once you have identified the amount of time a successful person would spend on activities which would lead to success in your specified goal, compare this with how much time you currently spend on those same activities. If your goal is academic success, how much time do you currently spend in study? If your goal is to be a good parent, how much time are you currently spending with your children?

It is important that your baseline or starting point is an accurate reflection of your situation. Our perceptions about ourselves can be tainted by our self-image to the point of deception. So for the 21 days, do nothing more than record faithfully the activities/actions you identified.

Reassess your goals

You now have a set of goals, a fairly good idea of what it takes to achieve those goals and, most importantly, you now have a more accurate picture of what it would take for you to achieve the particular goal. At this stage, you will have to decide whether you want to proceed or not. Whether you are prepared to make the sort of changes that are required in order for you to achieve your goal. For instance, if your career goal will require you to spend much more time on work activities at the expense of family time, you may not be prepared to make this change.

The main point is that you are now in a much better position to select, assess and define your goals.

Know how

Add the 'how' to your goals. How are you going to achieve your goals? Set up milestones, activities and action plans. Contrary to common goal setting practice, we believe you do not have to set these in great detail at the outset. Emphasis on detail at the outset is one of the key reasons why people abandon the process prematurely. Your milestones, action plans and activities will emerge and solidify during the process.

Choose your reinforcers

If you meet your daily goal, what reward will you allow yourself? Daily rewards might be watching television, a special food treat, socialising with friends. How will you reward yourself for reaching weekly, monthly, yearly goals?

Record your progress

Keep accurate records of the amount of time spent each day on the desired activity. Software programs like 'My Goals' greatly simplify this process.

Analyse your progress and make improvements

The secret of success lies not in quantum leaps but in gradual improvements over a period of time. Top athletes, corporations and even nations such as Japan have used this simple principle with great effect to achieve and maintain peak performance.

Reward your successes

If you meet your goals, milestones or complete activities then reward yourself. If you fall short, be honest with yourself and skip the reward.

Once you've reached your goal – set a new one.

Self-actualisation is not a destination but a journey.

Write a memo to yourself for future reference whenever you have completed a difficult task which is going to recur. You will benefit if you have made a written record of your mistakes and the lessons learned.

Create more balance in your life

Complete the following task.

How you spend your week

Working on the basis of 100 waking, available hours in a week, create two pie-charts of how your time is spent now, and the other of how you would *ideally* like it to be. (Don't worry about how to achieve the ideal just yet.)

How it is now

How I would like it to be

Make a list of the activities or tasks that you would like to do more in a typical week, and then the activities/tasks that you would like to do less.

Activities I want to decrease	Activities I would like to increase

Now, pick one item from each list and start to plan and make time for the favourite thing and find ways to overcome, reduce or drop the other. Review this list regularly and amend it accordingly.

Self-recording as a tool for self-development

Even if you find it difficult to find reinforcers or maintain the idea of rewarding or withholding rewards, don't worry, you are still likely to succeed. Simply knowing that you are reaching a desired goal can be reward enough. *The key to any self-management programme is accurate record-keeping.*

This is demonstrated by a study with students. One group recorded behaviour on a daily and weekly basis whilst the other group did not. Even though no extra rewards were offered, students who recorded their study time earned better grades than those who did not (Johnson & White 1981).

Behavioural contracting

If you are having problems sticking to your goals, you could try behavioural contracting to get some leverage in achieving your goal. You commit yourself to achieving a particular goal, the rewards, the privileges you will forfeit or punishments you must accept. To give you the leverage you commit to this contract by telling as many people who are close to you as you like.

Such a contract can be quite motivating, particularly when a mild punishment is part of the agreement. Here are two examples.

A student working on his PhD had trouble completing his final dissertation – for over two years he had not written a single page. A contract was drawn up for him which set out a timetable of activity which included completing a set number of pages each week. To make sure he kept to his timetable, he wrote post-dated cheques which would be posted each time he missed a deadline. The cheques were made out to organisations he despised (the Klu Klux Klan and American Nazi Party). He not only completed his dissertation but also his work output greatly increased.

The second example comes from Anthony Robbins' best-seller, *Awaken the Giant Within* and is called the Alpo Diet.

A woman and her friend had committed over and over again to losing weight, but failed to keep their promise every time. Finally, they both reached the point where losing weight was a must – they needed some leverage to push themselves over the edge. They needed to make ***not*** keeping their promise more painful than anything they could imagine.

They decided to commit to each other and a group of friends that if they welshed on their promise this time, they would each have to eat a whole can of Alpo dog food! So, to stave off any hint of a craving, these two enterprising women told everyone and kept their cans in plain view at all times as a constant reminder. She told me that when they started to feel hunger pangs, they'd pick up the can and read the label. With ingredients boasting 'horsemeat chunks', they found no difficulty in sticking to their commitment. They achieved their goal without a hitch!

Exercise – Goal setting 1

Use this form to structure your approach to something you want to have, be or do from your ideal chart and set it as a goal.

1. Write a clear description of your goal.

____

____

2. Date to be achieved by.

____

3. How realistic is this goal?

____

4. Identify a series of smaller goals with realistic timescales.

____

____

____

5. Describe your goal as if it has already been achieved.

____

____

6. Write down at least three reasons why you want to achieve this goal?

____

____

____

7. Where are you now in relation to where you want to be?

8. Make a list of things that you may need to achieve this goal.

9. Make a list of activities, which is organised by priorities.

10. Identify the obstacles that you may encounter.

11. How will you know when you have achieved this goal – what will you see, hear or experience?

12. Identify one thing that you can do today on this goal.

Exercise – Goal setting 2

Complete the following:

Name ______________________________

Daytime telephone/extension ______________________________

Today's date ______________________________

Write down **ONE** work related goal that you would like to achieve in the next 30 days.

It must be clear, specific, measurable and controllable at least in part, by you, and have a 50/50 chance of realistic success:

My goal is to...

____

____

____

Exercise – Goal setting 3

Describe yourself, your life, and the things around you in ten years' time:

____

____

____

____

____

____

Describe yourself, your life, and the things around you in five year's time:

Describe yourself, your life, and the things around you in one year's time:

Exercise – 90 day goal setting

Write down ten goals that you could aim to achieve in the next 90 days that would start you on the right path to achieving your long range goals:

1. ______________________________

2. ______________________________

3. ______________________________

4. ______________________________

5. ______________________________

6. ______________________________

7. ______________________________

8. ______________________________

9. ______________________________

10. ______________________________

Dealing with office interruptions

Why people interrupt you…
Interruption analysis
How to say 'not now' nicely: A three stage strategy
Creating the right environment: Get rid of the chair! • Look organised! • Get a big clock! Face away from the traffic flow • Learn how to close your door
Using non-verbal signals
How to become more assertive: Definition of assertion Situational versus generalised assertion • Aggression and non-assertion
Assertive techniques
Verbal assertion: Other ways of increasing assertion
Types of assertion – summary
No more nice guy! Recognising behaviour
Avoid interruptions
How to say 'NO' nicely: Saying no – some ideas
Learn to negotiate time scales
Dealing with your boss: Do unto others as you would be done by
Ruthless with time, gracious with people

Why people interrupt you…
Interruption analysis
How to say 'not now' nicely: A three stage strategy
Creating the right environment: Get rid of the chair! • Look organised! • Get a big clock!
Face away from the traffic flow • Learn how to close your door
Using non-verbal signals
How to become more assertive: Definition of assertion
Situational versus generalised assertion
Aggression and non-assertion
Assertive techniques
Verbal assertion: Other ways of increasing assertion

five

Why people interrupt you…

Regardless of whether you work in an open plan office or a closed door office, or even if you don't work in an office at all, if you get a great deal of face-to-face drop-in interruptions then the chances are that it is because of one or two things:

1. You have trained people and let them know that you can be interrupted at any time or
2. You are still holding onto tasks that you should have delegated.

There may be people in your organisation who cannot easily be interrupted, either because of their routine and their ability to communicate to people when not to interrupt them, or perhaps because it is known and understood that they don't like being disturbed. They may also have trained people how to handle certain situations or tasks so they no longer have to refer back to them for advice. We can learn from this and develop these skills for ourselves.

If you find it difficult to get any 'quiet time,' try to arrive at the office before anyone else to gain uninterrupted time for planning and other tasks.

Remember, nobody can interrupt you without your permission

If you accept for the moment that you have trained people to interrupt you, which may seem rather hard and unfair initially, eventually it is rather beneficial. This is because it means we can 'untrain' them or rather, train them to not interrupt us. We can also train them when we would rather not be interrupted when we are completely free to be interrupted

Different interruptions require different solutions

The two main considerations are:

- Who's interrupting you?
- What is the interruption about and how important/urgent is it?

Interruption analysis

Make a list of all your typical interruptions for a day or week on the following table, and rank each for importance, urgency and relevance. Alternatively, make a list of typical face-to-face or office interruptions that you encounter.

Time	Who	Subject	**Importance** High/Med/Low	**Urgency** High/Med/Low	**Relevance to me** High/Med/Low	**Could this have waited?**	**Could this have been handled by someone else?**

How to say 'NOT NOW' nicely

A three stage strategy

> If you find it hard to say 'No' or 'Go away' – saying 'Not now' is more realistic.

In dealing with face-to-face interruptions and drop-in visitors there is a simple, straightforward and very effective three point plan.

1. Prevent them, wherever possible, either in full or for a period of time during each and every day
2. Minimise their length of time, and
3. Reduce their distraction and destruction effect, bouncing back from them as quickly as you possibly can.

Many of the interruptions you receive may be legitimate requests for help, they may be necessary as part of your job. Indeed, if you are dealing with customers in a face-to-face environment it's probably written in your Job Description. You may also have other tasks to get on with. You can prevent interruptions by letting a colleague deal with them for a short time while you finish the other things. Or, you can prepare better and be more skilful at handling the interruptions so they can move more quickly, or if nothing else, when the interruption is dealt with, you can go back immediately to what you are working on rather than think, now, what shall I do next?

Creating the right environment

Get rid of the chair!

If you have a chair in front of your desk, for someone about to interrupt you this is a welcoming sign. It invites them to sit down in front of you, make themselves comfortable and settle down for a nice long chat or discussion. In some ways this is the most obvious and most blatant sign to anybody that you can be interrupted. It welcomes them in, makes the interruption perhaps take a little longer than it should do and makes it even more difficult for you to get them out of the way from your desk, work area or office.

So, simply get rid of the chair from your desk or move it out of your office completely. If you decide you need to have a chair then put it to the side of the room away from the desk, make it a rather uncomfortable formal chair and not one that people can get too comfortable in. If necessary, and this is probably the one time that it is ever wise to be cluttered, put things on the chair to hinder people sitting down.

Look organised!

Establish your lowest productivity hours as 'interruptions' hours. Encourage your subordinates to see you then.

An organised busy person whose work area gives off the signals that they are going somewhere and are on a bit of a mission, will also communicate a sense of urgency and non-interruptibility to any potential drop-in visitors. Of course, we are not trying to scare all the drop-in visitors away – many of the interruptions may be welcome or more important than the task we are working on.

One of the things that we want to make clear to people is that we are busy and we only prefer to be interrupted by the most important things. Make sure that your work area is organised, tidy, efficient and that you represent somebody who is effective.

Get a big clock!

There is nothing like a nice big clock on your office wall to signal to people that you consider time to be of value. I remember seeing a big clock, sitting prominently on a manager's wall. It had the words inscribed on it in big red letters **KILL TIME AND YOU MURDER SUCCESS**.

Set your clock to run five minutes fast, this allows you to be slightly early for meetings.

I sat in the manager's office watching people interrupt him from time to time, at certain points in the conversation he would use very subtle non-verbal signals of quickly glancing at the clock. People unconsciously got the message that they needed to get to the point and leave. It wasn't rude, in fact it was extremely polite, because of its non-verbal understated manner. If nothing else, have a clock on your desk in front of you.

- Use it to draw attention to time passing, non-verbally
- It show people you value your time
- It helps you to develop a sense of time
- Use it to agree time-limits to meetings and conversations

Face away from the traffic flow

One of the easiest and surest ways to interrupt, is to make eye contact, for example.

Try this tomorrow when one of your colleagues is on the phone with somebody, wait until the middle of the conversation, look across the room and make eye contact with them and simply wave and say 'hello'. They will probably make eye contact back and wave saying 'hello' and then realise that they have completely forgotten who they are talking to and what has just been said.

If you really want to avoid an interruption don't look up and make eye contact.

If you work in an open plan office make sure that your desk or work area faces the screen or looks away from people walking towards you.

If people walk up to your desk with work or an interruption, just pause before you look up – maybe continuing to work that little bit longer – it will indicate to them that you are busy and that you don't give your attention too easily or freely.

Learn how to close your door

Many managers who have the luxury of a 'cell type' office with a door that they can close don't like to close the door for one simple reason, they like to feel that the door is *always* open!

Learn to close the door. If you don't like to close it completely just close the door so that it is only just open. This will signal to people that you are busy and just require them to hesitate and double think whether their interruption is really important or whether it can wait.

Using non-verbal signals

I remember visiting the office of one chief executive of a large organisation. Outside his executive suite next to the door were three coloured lights: red, orange and green. From a panel on his desk he could set a signal as for his readiness for interruptions, a red light would mean only if the building is burning down, an orange light meant it had better be important, and the green light meant come on in for anybody and anything. Well, this may be a little extreme and a little extravagant for most of us, but the lesson is to learn how to give signals to people that you are not available for interruption at certain times of the day.

For example, some companies, particularly those who work with a shop floor environment or an open plan environment, find that they can wear something that gives people the signal. One large supermarket chain went out and equipped their managers with hundreds of red baseball caps. The instruction was that these managers could wear the red baseball cap at any time during the day for up to 60 minutes if they did not want to be interrupted, they became nicknamed 'the thinking caps'.

Schedule regular, routine meetings at common points during the day to discuss things, thus avoiding non-urgent interruptions.

You might also consider using a sign such as 'Do Not Disturb' on your door. This might work, although frequently, after a period of time, this might be ignored. If this is the case then try something stronger, perhaps 'Interview in Progress' or 'Manager in Therapy'!

Another 'signal' which is even more unusual but a rather riskier strategy, and therefore only best used in extreme situations, is this. Arrive in the morning with the worst, most bad tempered expression your face. Storm through the office, sit down at your desk and say nothing. It will probably be a good two hours before anybody summons up the courage to interrupt you!

Perhaps the clearest signal of all is that of proactive communication. Tell people when you can and cannot be interrupted.

How to become more assertive

Definition of assertion

Self expression through which one stands up for his or her basic human rights without violating the basic human rights of others.

Situational versus generalised assertion

There are no assertive, non-assertive, or aggressive people – only assertive non-assertive responses to situations. It is useful to look at these behaviours not as 'good' or 'bad', but as more or less helpful or desirable. Situational non-assertion means that the response is not part of an overriding pattern (generalised non-assertion or aggression) but occurs only in certain types of situations. It is not the result of a deep emotional problem, and basic interpersonal skills are not lacking. In the case of situational non-assertiveness we may assume we are dealing with a relatively healthy person who wishes to develop new ways of handling situations which are now uncomfortable, self-denying and non-adaptive for them. If they did nothing about these situations, they would still be able to function in a relatively healthy manner.

Aggression and non-assertion

Aggression and non-assertion are response styles that tend to hide the real message a person wishes to send. A person who habitually uses a non-assertive response in a given situation may build up resentments until they burst out in a flash of aggression; or they might act aggressively toward a person over whom they feel more power.

People may respond aggressively in situations because of an accumulation of bad feelings, frustration, a transfer of reactions to past emotional experiences into the present and a belief that only aggression will work.

In the long run, both non-assertion and aggression result in a loss. Non-assertion rarely helps people get what they want or lets others know how they feel, and it also shows a subtle lack of respect for the other person's ability to take disappointments, to shoulder some responsibility, to handle their own problems. Non-asserters often discount themselves by thinking that what they have to say is not important enough. Non-assertive respondents must realise that small points are not necessarily unimportant ones. An aggressive response often results in long-term loss of friendship and even of the original goal because others find a way to get back at the person who has acted aggressively.

Assertive people can express anger, but in doing so they direct anger at the behaviour or issue, not at the person, and lets it be known exactly what is desired without trying to dominate, humiliate, or insult the other person. Sometimes people skirt the border between aggression and non-assertion with an indirect, mixed response that seems non-assertive but the effect on others is the same as an aggressive response. This is sometimes known as 'indirect aggression'. A person appears to go along with what another says, but in reality they have the definite goal of being aggressive. The methods used may range from guilt induction to sabotage.

There are also times when the person to whom an assertive response is directed does not know how to stand up for his/her own rights and make a response in kind. In such a situation, the asserter has the responsibility to ascertain as clearly as possible what the other person's position is, rather than simply taking advantage by making assumptions about the feelings of the unskilled person. The underlying philosophy of assertion is humanistic and aimed at a win-win solution.

Reasons for assertion

- It is respectful of both oneself and others.
- It usually leads to better feelings on both sides.
- It gives a person more control over the behaviour.
- It usually 'works' better than non-assertion or aggression.
- It provides a win-win result.
- It means increased calm.
- It helps one to communicate what one is, feels, thinks and wants.
- It helps to let others know the 'real' you and you to know the 'real' them.

Why people choose not to be assertive

- Risks too great – not worth time or energy.
- Costs to other person outweigh benefits of assertion.
- Other person has already changed behaviour appropriately.
- Situation does not warrant an assertive response.

Assertive techniques

It is something you can improve. Our culture is not good at encour aging assertiveness – we fear being seen as pushy.

Three steps to assertiveness

1. Vision – what do I want out of it?
2. Planning – prepare responses (how, when and if)
3. Practice – keep trying and learning

Verbal assertion

Active assertion

- Stating demands
- Repetition
- Seeking criticism
- Standing up for your rights

Passive assertion

- Acknowledging criticism
- Handling manipulation
- Agreeing with criticism
- Self-disclosure

Stating demands model

1. Evaluate positively and/or negatively
2. State expectations
3. Offer incentive and/or pressure

In the stating demands model (above) it is essential to use all three elements. Many people use evaluation but do a poor job stating goals, which leaves the other unclear as to what is wanted from them. Stating expectations is the core of the stating demands model.

Evaluation and the incentives or pressures are most effective when they specify consequences which ***you*** control. The distinction between evaluation and incentives and pressures is that evaluation refers to past behaviour, whereas incentives refer to future behaviour. It should also be stressed that stating demands is more effective if reasons for justification are avoided.

Other ways of increasing assertion

Repetition

A technique for saying what you want over and over and over again that helps you develop persistence without being side-tracked into argument or justification regarding your demands.

Seeking criticism

A technique that reduces others manipulative ploys by actively eliciting negative feedback.

Acknowledging criticism

A technique that teaches acceptance of manipulative criticism by calmly acknowledging to your critic the possibility that there may be some truth in what they have said.

Agreeing with criticism

A technique that reduces other's manipulation by expressing acceptance of your shortcomings, through sympathetically agreeing with hostile or constructive criticism of your negative qualities.

Self-disclosure

A technique that reduces manipulation by others, through disclosure of both positive and negative aspects of your personality, behaviour and lifestyle.

Assertion reducers

Do less of these if you want to improve your ability to assert your rights to not be needlessly interrupted at an inconvenient time.

1. Argument dilution
2. Excuses/lies
3. Qualifiers
4. Personal attacks and losing your temper
5. Psychological manipulation (including using guilt, praise or making the other person feel anxious or ignorant)
6. Non-verbal music (excessive movement or fidgeting)
7. Withdrawing (avoiding the situation or raising the issue)

Most of these are fairly self explanatory, however, here are notes on qualifiers:

Qualifiers: Don't overqualify statements

We are often apprehensive about how a message will be received and in order to soften its impact we qualify our thoughts or feelings. Qualifiers are words or phrases that weaken your message:

- 'I hope you don't mind, but... '
- 'I hope I'm not bothering you, but... '
- 'I may be wrong, but... '

The common element in all these qualifiers is the word 'but', which serves to discredit everything in the sentence that precedes it. In fact, when used often enough, the mere sound of 'but' serves as a warning that the forthcoming words will totally contradict what has already been said: 'We've found your work here quite satisfactory, but our budget forces us to let you go.' 'The paper you wrote in this exam had several good ideas, but I graded it as a D.'

Other qualifiers include:

- Just (as in 'I just wanted to talk to you for a few minutes,' or 'There's just one problem… ')
- Kind of, sort of (as in 'I was kind of unhappy about what you said about me,' or 'I sort of hope you can keep the noise down')
- Any type of apology (such as 'I'm sorry to bring this up,' or 'I hate to ask this favour')

You can see from these few examples that in overusing qualifiers you become your own worst enemy, discounting everything you've said before the other person even responds.

Remember: You have the right to appear foolish, to be unsure of yourself, to express your feelings and to act independently of the approval of others. Don't apologise for yourself: There's nothing wrong with your thoughts! Take yourself seriously and others will start to do the same thing. This suggestion doesn't mean that you should totally remove qualifiers from your language. Of course there are times when you ought to apologise for your actions or express your uncertainty, but don't overdo it or your image will suffer, both in your own eyes and in the eyes of others.

Types of assertion – summary

Type	Definition	Example
Basic	A straightforward statement that stands up for your rights by making clear your needs, wants, beliefs, opinions or feelings.	I don't really have time now, let's meet tomorrow at… and do it then.
Empathetic	A behaviour that contains an element of empathy as well as a statement of needs and wants.	I know you're busy at the moment too, and that this is important, and as I really don't have time now, let's meet tomorrow at… and do it properly then.
Responsive	A behaviour that aims to find out where the other person stands, their needs, wants, opinions and feelings.	How long does this take? Can we cover it in ten minutes? Have you tried tackling this yourself at all?
Discrepancy.	A statement that points out the difference between what has previously been agreed, and what is actually happening or about to happen.	I remember you saying that you would check with me before you make offers to candidates, I would still like you to do that.
Negative feelings	A statement that draws the attention of another person to the undesirable effect that their behaviour is having on you. It can contain the following elements: When… I feel… I'd like…	When you interrupt it means that I end up doing two things half as well. I would prefer it if you could store things up so that we can go through them properly.
Consequence	A statement that informs the other person of the consequences for them of not changing their behaviour. It also gives them an opportunity to change their behaviour.	If you continue to need help on this project, then I shall have to direct to someone else, as I really do not have enough time to spare myself.

No more nice guy!

Recognising behaviour

Imagine that your behavioural response to another person can be placed on a scale, with passive behaviour at one end and aggressive behaviour at the other, assertive is in the middle of that scale.

Aggressive behaviour is generally held to be unacceptable in our culture. This unusually means that when we choose not to be assertive, we move along the scale towards passive behaviour. This often results in being nice to everybody except ourselves. Think of the times when we have said something like; 'OK, leave it with me, I'll sort it out... ' only because we don't know what else to say or do.

Practise the methods suggested below until they become natural and acceptable to you.

Voice

Non-assertive	Assertive	Aggressive
■ Wavering	■ Steady and firm	■ Very firm
■ Tone may be singing or whining	■ Tone is middle range, rich and warm	■ Tone is sarcastic sometimes cold
■ Over-soft or over-warm	■ Sincere and clear	■ Hard and sharp
■ Often dull and monotone. Quiet, often drops away at end	■ Not over-loud or quiet	■ Strident, maybe shouting, rises at end

Speech

Non-assertive	Assertive	Aggressive
■ Hesitant and filled with pauses	■ Fluent, few awkward hesitances	■ Fluent, few awkward hesitances
■ Sometimes jerks from fast to slow	■ Emphases key words	■ Often abrupt, clipped
■ Frequent throat clearing	■ Steady, even pace	■ Emphases blaming words
		■ Often fast

Facial

Non-assertive	Assertive	Aggressive
■ 'Ghosts' smiles when expressing anger, or being criticised	■ Smiles when pleased	■ Smile may becomes 'wry'
■ Eyebrows raised in anticipation (eg of rebuke)	■ Frowns when angry otherwise 'open'	■ Scowls when angry
■ Quick-changing features	■ Features steady	■ Eyebrows raised in amazement/disbelief
■ Jaw relaxed	■ Jaw set firm	■ Chin thrust forward

Eyes

Non-assertive	Assertive	Aggressive
■ Evasive	■ Firm but not a 'stare down'	■ Tries to stare down and dominate

Body

Non-assertive	Assertive	Aggressive
■ Hand-wringing	■ Open hand movements (inviting to speak)	■ Finger pointing
■ Hunching shoulders	■ Measured pace/hand movements	■ Fist thumping
■ Stepping back	■ Sits upright or relaxed (not slouching or cowering)	■ Sits upright or leans forward
■ Covering mouth with hand	■ Stands with head held up	■ Stands upright head 'in air'
■ Nervous movements which distract (shrugs and shuffles)		■ Strides around (impatiently)
■ Arms crossed low for protection		■ Arms crossed high (unapproachable)

Avoid interruptions

Find an office somewhere and go and 'hide' for an hour.

You may find, or believe that some of the interruptions you get are simply because people know you are there. The source of the interruption may be things that they should be dealing with themselves, but because in the past they have often come to you for your assistance, they keep coming to you. You need to wean them off this and give them the confidence and maybe the habit of doing it themselves.

Try being unavailable for a short period of time. Tell them that while you are gone they should deal with things as best they can and to let you know how they got on when you return. So long as the person can do the job or task well, it should only be a matter of their confidence and habit that you need to instil in them.

How to say 'NO' nicely

Many people don't like saying **NO** to a request for assistance or help. This is understandable, we all like to help people. Not only does it give us a sense of self-importance and self-justification but it is also satisfying when we get praise and appreciation. However, these are slim rewards when we find ourselves drowning in an ever increasing work load with less and less time to achieve and do things. At this point we must be able to find ways to say **NO** nicely, in a way that protects self-esteem, makes them realise we are not saying no to them as an individual, but also allows us to deflect the interruption and get on with what we are doing.

Saying NO – some ideas

1. Whenever you say **NO**, give a reason as to why not. By stating a reason you will allow the other person to justify to themselves that it is not them you are rejecting, it is just their interruption.
2. When you say **NO**, you really mean not *now*. This should encourage people to save things up for you as well. Begin to develop expressions such as 'I can't really deal with that now because I am trying to get this finished, but what I will do is come and find you at about 4 o'clock, OK?'
3. Whenever you say what you can't do, say what you can do. This ends a sentence or a command on a positive note and has a much lower tendency to invite someone to challenge it. Consider this interchange – a colleague comes up to you and asks you to look over some figures with them prior to a meeting they are having tomorrow. You simply blurt out 'No, I can't deal with this now.' This may then lead to them insisting how important it is and how vital your input is, increasing the pressure on you to give in. Instead of that, say to them 'I can't deal with that now but what I can do is I can ask Colin to give you a hand and he should be able to explain them.' Or, 'I can't deal with that now but I can find you in about half an hour when I have finished.' Either of these types of responses are preferable to leaving it on a negative.

4. When you say 'No' sound like you mean it. Many people when they are trying to be assertive use a very soft tone of voice or put a lot of softeners into their speech pattern. For example, you might say, 'Look, I am really sorry I've got to get this finished, would it be possible to come and find you a little bit later, will that be OK?' The person is subconsciously alerted that, by asking your permission and approval, you may be persuaded to be interrupted if they just give you a little more of a prompt and a little more resistance. Contrast this with the expression – 'No, I need to get this finished now. I'll come and find you later, OK?' You might want to try – 'Can I come and find you later, OK.' But in this example you will notice there is no question mark at the end of the sentence. Verbally you would do this by making your voice tone go down, even give more dip in tone at the end of the sentence. This will turn what seems to be a question (it starts with 'could I') into an actual command.
5. When you promise to come and find somebody later, turn to your diary and write it in either a time slot or on a To-do list. Both of these will indicate to the person that you are serious about keeping your promise and make them realise that you are not simply dismissing them.
6. Use your plan, schedule or diary as the reason why you can't deal with the interruption now. Have your diary out in front of you, point to the next activity you have scheduled, if you have a blank diary with nothing written in it, this is not very convincing. If you have a diary with time scheduled then you can point to the gaps you have left in the diary and say 'I will come and find you at 3.30 when I have finished preparing for tomorrow's Board Meeting'. This, once again, will alert people to the way you work and instead of interrupting you, they will actually begin to approach you and say 'I need to have a word with you later, when would be a good time?' This happens surprisingly quickly, after just a few times, and people soon get the message. It *is* possible to train people to interrupt you less.

Of course, it is important that when you do deflect people, you do follow up and see what their point is. The solution to so many face-to-face interruptions is to visit them at ***your*** convenience.

It is much easier to control the timescale of an interruption when you are at *their* desk because you can walk away. You can choose to stand up or sit down (it's very difficult to get people to walk away from your desk).

In very difficult cases, you might try some of the measures (outlined below) all of which have proved successful in dealing with face-to-face drop-in interruptions, perhaps of a more persistent variety.

As someone walks towards you and you catch sight of them out of the corner of your eye quickly pick up the phone and make as if you are on the telephone. Perhaps you could have your secretary/assistant put a call through to you after a few minutes, ask the person if you can come and find them later because this call is rather important and you need to take it now. Of course, the call may be no more than the speaking clock or dialling tone.

When the person walks towards you stand up and meet them in front of your desk or half way down the corridor, hold the discussion standing up (this will invariably shorten the talk) and then stroll back to your work area promising to come and see them later.

Buy yourself an egg timer. Next time somebody comes up to you and says have you got a minute say 'Yes, you can have three!', turn the egg timer over and watch the sand go through. This may be a shock to people but the important thing is that you put a time limit to the interruption. If you have to deal with the interruption because it is your boss or because it is your job, make it clear that you are working to a timescale and state what that timescale is, whether it is five, ten or 30 minutes. Perhaps when you accept an interruption simply say, 'OK. I've got a call to make/somewhere to go/something to start at 3 o'clock, we have until then.'

Learn to negotiate timescales

Whilst you may not be able to dispute the importance of an activity – we often find that things delegated down from our boss, manager or supervisor, have an importance rating all of their own – it is usually possible to negotiate the timescale within which that task has to be completed.

Always arrange to go and meet others at their desk – you will have more control and typically the discussion will be shorter.

A good example of this is when the customer requests our attention. Clearly it is not good customer service or smart business practice to say 'No' whenever a customer asks for something. In fact, as you know, the customer is nearly always right. Even if they are not, they are always the customer and what we need to do is to develop the skills of being able to negotiate the timescales.

In most activities there are two deadlines. The first is when something ideally needs to be done; this is considered to be the first goal post. The second is the last time by which it has to be done. This is the second goal post. When somebody asks you to complete something or do something for them you could instigate the following dialogue:

'When would you like this ideally done by?'

'Tomorrow afternoon,'

'OK, what sort of time?'

'Oh I don't know, any time before 5.00pm.'

'OK, what is the absolute latest time you need to have it by?'

They may respond by saying that they actually need to have it on Friday because that's when their meeting is.

You now have a very clear understanding of what they mean when they say, 'This is urgent, I have to have this done quickly' – or that terrible expression – 'As soon as possible.'

The term, 'As soon as possible', apart from causing untold stress, communicates very little about when somebody expects to have something completed. Take two people asking for things to be done as soon as possible, one may require it in minutes, the other in hours and the chances are that at every guess we will get it wrong.

Dealing with your boss

Perhaps one of the most difficult interruptions of all to deal with is that of your boss or manager. Clearly it may not be a good career move to become too assertive or too controlling in dealing with the interruption.

However, we can strike a balance between maintaining a good working relationship and being productive. Many people have found that one successful strategy for controlling the interruptions from your manager is this, before you begin a piece of work or activity that requires no interruptions, go to see them and ask if there is anything they need you to work on before you start. Get a clear commitment – yes or no. Then tell them that you are starting the activity now, that you will be about an hour and that you will find them when you have finished to see if they need anything. Check that this will be all right, gain their commitment again and go on.

If they do still come up to you, show them a nice clear in-tray and ask them to leave it there for you to look at the minute you have finished. In this way you can begin to train them that you are as organised and as efficient as perhaps they would like to be.

Arrange one or two fixed times of the day when you and your boss can meet for a pre-determined length of time to discuss what has arisen.

Do unto others as you would be done by

Clearly one of the ways to set standard behaviour is to lead by example.

If you would like to be interrupted less then make sure that you don't interrupt other people any more than you have to.

Ruthless with time, gracious with people

In all these different ways of controlling face-to-face interruptions there is one principle. It is this, be gracious with people and ruthless with time.

If you do accept an unplanned interruption, agree a time limit with the other person; 'OK, only if we can cover it in ten minutes or less.'

People are one of your greatest resources to help you achieve the things that you need to and to make your organisation work. Any disruption to good relationships between people will, in the long-term, be counter protective. Indeed, all these ideas should lead to better and more understanding relationships with colleagues by showing your need to get on and do things without interruption and by respecting other people's needs for the same.

Dealing with telephone interruptions

Don't ask people to call you back: No more delay and frustration

Give call back times

Batch calls together

Prepare for effective telephone conversations

Make notes when you are on the telephone

Stand up whilst you are making telephone calls

Time your telephone calls

Use a call divert for one hour a day: Divert your calls today

Screen calls effectively

Further application points: Personal improvement summary

Don't ask people to call you back: No more delay and frustration

Give call back times

Batch calls together

Prepare for effective telephone conversations

Make notes when you are on the telephone

Stand up whilst you are making telephone calls

Time your telephone calls

Use a call divert for one hour a day: Divert your calls today

Screen calls effectively

Further application points: Personal improvement summary

Don't ask people to call you back: No more delay and frustration

Give call back times

Batch calls together

Prepare for effective telephone conversations

Make notes when you are on the telephone

Stand up whilst you are making telephone calls

six

Don't ask people to call you back

In the same way that you may have trained people that you can be interrupted in a face-to-face environment, you will have unwittingly instructed people to interrupt you by telephone.

We probably do it out of habit without realising how. It is common experience that when business people try to contact each other, the chances of them finding them at the end of the telephone is less then 50 per cent.

What does this mean? It means that 50 per cent of the telephone calls that you make will probably result in the person:

- Not being there
- Screening their calls
- In a meeting or
- On the telephone themselves.

This leaves you a choice of two actions.

1. **For you to call them back**

2. **For them to call you back.**

There may be a possible alternative. Putting the information on the fax or leaving a clear message. However, whenever you ask somebody to call you back what you are actually doing is creating an interruption.

It will also catch you unprepared and very often you may forget why you asked them to call you back in the first place. This may then lead to either a wasted call or you putting them on hold while you try and find your notes or information.

Invite people to call you back when you know that you will be working on low-priority tasks or available to take calls. Have their details to hand.

Seven ways to control telephone time bandits

1. Reduce telephone interruptions to an absolute minimum where possible; remember, not every call is an urgent, high-priority call (*remember the 80/20 rule?*)
2. Minimise the distraction factor.
3. Reduce the length of each call.
4. Replace long calls with fax or e-mail.
5. Avoid mistakes and duplication of effort by taking notes.
6. Use the telephone to save time in face-to-face meetings and letter writing.
7. Make and take longer calls away from peak or prime times or in 'opportunity' time.

No more delay and frustration

So instead simply follow these steps:

- Where appropriate, leave a message that you called.
- Ask the person who answered the telephone when the person you are calling is expected back.
- Get a time; if they say that they will be back in tomorrow ask the operator when would be a good time to call.
- Give a reason why they can't call you, such as, 'I shall be in a meeting…', 'travelling', or try this phrase, 'I work from an outgoing diary… ' This will minimise and reduce the chance of you actually missing them again.

This approach may take a little discipline to succeed, but it works extremely well for both internal and external customers. External customers do not seem to understand why they should call you back, so they actually prefer you to call them back.

This process will also avoid the game of 'telephone tag' – you call someone and leave a message for them to call you back. They then call you back only to find that you have just gone to lunch. On your return, you call them back. They have now gone to lunch and so the game goes on.

Never, never go on hold for more than 30 seconds. It only encourages companies to do it more, and it wastes your time and money.

Break the chain by simply not asking people to call you back but finding out when would be the best time to contact them. Schedule this call in your diary and then you will not forget it.

Give call back times

Ask yourself: Can I delegate this call? Ask them to call someone else!

There may be times where you do need to give people the opportunity to call you back. Or perhaps you prefer not to have too many outgoing calls for whatever reason.

If this is the case then adopt this principle absolutely. Whenever you try and contact somebody who is not there, simply leave a message that you have called, and ask them to give you a call at a set time.

This will allow you to channel most of your telephone interruptions into certain parts of the day, or the times which are less busy for you.

Of course, if the issue that they needed to contact you about was really important, they will probably phone earlier anyway. But if you say that you will not be available until that time they could find somebody else to help.

In 99.9 per cent of cases this works extremely well (with external customers where customer service is paramount, where this technique has been adopted and followed through in customer research).

Keep a note in your address book or diary of what is the best time to call different people. Also note those that can be called early or late in the day.

Customers perceive they are getting a higher level of personal service. The perception is that the customer service operator is trying even harder to accommodate the needs and wants of the customer. Leave accurate information as to when to call back and when to get hold of them. It is considered much more useful than having to play the game of telephone tag, being put on hold, passed around etc. You can, of course, then be prepared for the call back and have the relevant information to hand.

Batch calls together

By taking account of the ideas above you will, or should have slightly more outgoing calls to make. This, however, is not a time problem. By initiating the calls, you will probably have a higher level of control. You can decide whether to come to the point directly or have more small talk.

However, one of the greatest time savings can be simply batching calls together. Create time in your schedule at different points during the day to do all your telephone calls at once.

There are also other things you can do to shorten your telephone conversations without impacting either your relationships or effectiveness in communicating clearly.

Here are some of the best and most time effective methods to use when working through your batch of outgoing calls:

1. Have a list of the people to call with their telephone numbers written alongside the list. Make sure you have the list in front of you when you 'phone.

2. Pick up the receiver and do not replace the hand-piece in between calls. Simply click on the un-hook button and dial the next number. Click, dial the next number. Continue down your list until you have reached the bottom. If you have time, go back and contact or re-call anybody who was engaged or not available.
3. Do not allow yourself to be put on hold for longer than 30 seconds. Make the calls as brief and to the point as possible, at least until your objective is achieved. If you have time and you so wish allow time for any small talk or peripheral discussions.
4 If you are really tight for time let people know when you are actually making the call. Start your telephone conversation with something like 'This is a quick call, I'm just about to go into a meeting etc... I just want to check a few details... '

If you adopt these principles when making outgoing calls you will find them very effective in getting more calls done or the same number of calls in less time.

Preparing for effective telephone conversations

Whether you make more outgoing or incoming calls, preparation is a definite way of saving time. One example would be if you work in a customer service situation and need to answer and react to incoming customer queries and enquiries.

If you were to analyse these enquiries you would probably find that most of the calls you get are about a small number of issues. You will hear the same questions and queries repeated throughout the day. This is the **Pareto**

Create 'Cheat Sheets' of commonly asked questions or queries. These should be kept to hand, ideally in plastic wallets. Whenever you are asked something that you don't know, find out and add it to a Cheat Sheet.

Principle at work again, and can allow you to prepare the most important or the most commonly asked questions or problems in advance of the 'phone ringing.

Always make sure you have helpful information relating to these top items at hand. You don't actually have to have every piece of information ready, but just the ones ready that are most commonly encountered.

If you have to explain the same thing over and over again, then perhaps it would be an advantage to actually write down the expression, statements or questions that you could use, making sure that it is practised, concise and understandable.

> Remember that the person who makes the call has the psychological 'right' to terminate it. It is better to ring back so that you have that right.

For example, one company operating a large call centre handling telephone responses on a free 'phone number following advertising would brief its staff carefully on the contents of the advert, and what were the most common points or questions that people will ask. Armed with this information written in front of them, the telephonists could quickly offer clear explanations both to the delight of their customers and of course to themselves. The benefits of this included being able to handle far more calls with fewer operators, because each call was significantly shorter than if they were answered in an unstructured or unprepared way.

If you are making outgoing calls, no matter what the content of the telephone call, prepare carefully by making sure that you have notes and files to hand in front of you, details of any previous telephone conversations you may have had with that person and maybe some notes on your objectives or agenda points that you would like to raise.

Increasingly the telephone is replacing face-to-face meetings with customers and colleagues alike. In just the same way you might prepare for a face-to-face meeting, prepare for a telephone meeting.

Do not be afraid to schedule exact times of when to call people. Log it in your diary and it will remind you to make that call when the time/day arrives.

Make notes when you are on the telephone

One of the keys to becoming effective in what you do is to think more on paper. Whether this is in planning, jotting things down that you don't want to forget, making notes following meetings, discussions or telephone calls or confirming key details in writing.

Replace scraps of paper and 'Post-It' notes with proper message pads and notebooks. If it saves one lost message a year it's worth it.

One of the disadvantages of using the telephone is that sometimes the communication is very brief and may seem a little inexact. As you go through a telephone call be sure to make notes of the key conversation points as they occur (ideally in a notebook).

This also has the benefit of helping you concentrate, making sure that your eye contact does not wander off somewhere else. At the end of the telephone conversation simply review your notes out loud with the other person, checking the details that you have written down. Always be sure to read back and double check telephone numbers, dates, times, addresses and so on.

By keeping track and keeping files of notebooks in this way, you can actually refer back to previous conversations and double check details.

Stand up whilst you are making telephone calls

Apart from the physical benefits of stretching your legs and limbs after probably too many hours sitting down in an office, you may find that standing up during telephone calls actually makes the call shorter, perhaps through unconsciously willing it.

Slow your voice down on the telephone and **always** ask people to repeat numbers and important details, and then repeat it back to them. This can prevent delay or inconvenience in trying to sort out a misunderstanding.

You may often see people stand up automatically (or subconsciously) during telephone calls if the call requires them to concentrate or sound more confident, or if the caller is being particularly difficult. The fact is that your voice sounds different when you are standing up.

Somebody on the telephone can usually subconsciously hear how you are sitting or standing. If you are slumped over your desk doing something else, perhaps typing on the computer, they will certainly hear that.

If you are lying back in your chair with your feet on the desk that also gives a different tone to your voice. By standing up, your diaphragm opens up, your head goes back and typically the voice resonates slightly deeper.

Time your telephone calls

When you make or receive telephone calls do so with a clock in front of you, or possibly even an egg timer, to see if you can get off the 'phone and finish the call before the sand runs out. Just being more aware of time passing can actually make you unconsciously come to the point quicker, explain things more concisely and more thoroughly making each call slightly quicker.

Remember if you could save an average of one minute per telephone call, with the number of calls you make in a day, that could be half an hour to 45 minutes per day perhaps longer (one minute is not much of a saving and most people can improve their telephone communications by a greater degree).

Of course, you may not need to make telephone calls at all. Information can either be faxed or you may have other people who you can delegate telephone call-backs to.

Use a call divert for one hour a day

Just in the same way that people feel guilty about closing their office door, people sometimes feel guilty about switching on the answerphone or putting calls on divert. There is no need to feel guilty at all, so long as you actually return calls promptly and don't use the facility to simply avoid taking unpleasant calls or responsibility or use the facility to block calls.

An hour of time with the 'phone not ringing is a golden hour in which you can get things done. The telephone tends to demand our attention. A telephone has an unspecified sense of urgency.

We usually, mistakenly, believe that whenever the telephone rings, it is something urgent and important. In most cases neither of these things are true.

Divert your calls today

If you do not have any of the technology systems available to you, such as answerphones or voice mail, then try developing a body system. Have a colleague take your calls for say 30 to 60 minutes while you complete something else, and then you can later return the favour.

Many people sit at their desks working with a 'phone on divert or on answerphone. Do not feel guilty about doing this. It is a good and effective method in helping you become more productive.

Screen calls effectively

If you have the luxury of an assistant or colleague to screen your calls, here are some tips to help them do this more effectively.

1. Always ask who is calling and what it is regarding before checking to see if you are available.
2. Ask the caller polite questions such as, 'Will they know why you are calling?' or 'What is the purpose of your call?' etc.
3. If the call is a sales call, suggest that the sales person write in the first instance and call back at a specified time. You may find it useful to assign an hour every single week where you have a 'free for all' 'phone in. This is the one hour that your secretary or assistant can invite sales people to call. You may be surprised how many people don't, given the opportunity. Of course, if they do, they get put straight through.
4. If possible, re-direct the call to somebody else in the office or building who the caller could speak to initially, or who is better able to handle the query.
5. Try to avoid too many clichéd 'they are in a meeting' type expressions. Instead, have the assistant take control of the call by saying 'I cannot put you through, they are not available at the moment, can I take your number and pass the details on to them?'
6. Do not allow your secretary or assistant to make promises that you may not want to keep, like promising to call people back or do things. Have them use expressions such as, 'I will ask him to call you back' or 'I will ask them to do this for you when they come back in the office.'
7. Always remember to be polite when screening any type of call, showing respect for the person's self-esteem. Even if it might be the twentieth sales person you have had on that morning they have a legitimate job to do, but just make sure they are actually contacting the right person and re-direct them if necessary
8. Be honest and say whether you are interested in sales people or not. Don't simply ask them to put something in the post to get them off the 'phone. Invariably they may take this as being interested in their proposition and follow it up.

If you do not have an assistant or work on your own – use an answerphone as a 'call screening device'. Record a new topical message daily and pick up any important calls during the recording session.

Further application points

1. Log all telephone calls for a typical day. Note the number of incoming vs. outgoing calls, and the percentage of people not available. Also log the average length of each call. Repeat this exercise every 6-8 weeks.
2. Experiment with telephoning regular contacts at different times of the day. Are the calls shorter and more effective?
3. Make some time to read through your instruction manual for your telephone system – can you operate all the different functions confidently?
4. Is your internal telephone directory up-to-date?
5. Review your call log and ask:
   - Which calls took too long?
   - Which calls where low priority?
   - Were there any calls that could have been handled by someone else?
   - How many calls where mis-routed?
   - How many times did you get put on hold?
   - How many calls interrupted something more important?

Personal improvement summary

Take a moment to make notes on each of these topics:

Is this you?	What you can do about it
1. I am frequently interrupted during meetings and conversations with telephone calls.	
2. I subscribe to a 'call waiting' service.	
3. I forget to return calls.	
4. I find myself losing or mislaying telephone messages or telephone numbers.	
5. I find myself finishing calls and then forget some key point or question that I meant to discuss.	
6. I find myself sitting on hold during peak times during the day. I may have to call some people three or four times to get hold of them.	
7. I find myself talking to people about relatively trivial matters for too long.	
8. I find it difficult to get people off the phone when I want to get on with something.	

The three most important changes I can make are:

Conquering the paperwork battle

When in doubt throw it out: Personal organisation quiz

Keep a clear desk

Dejunk your desk

Fantastic filing

The ten commandments of e-mail: Some golden rules

Improve note taking with mind maps: Why use mind maps? • Drawing basic mind maps • Improving your mind maps • Summary

Active reading: Read quicker and more effectively

Knowing what you want to know: Knowing how deeply to study the material • Speed reading magazines and newspapers: Article types and how to read them • Deal with mail effectively • Read technical information effectively Reading 'whole subject' documents

Improving reading speed: Improvement of reading rate Summary

SQ3R: Survey, Question, Read, Recall and Review

Communicate information quickly and effectively: Targeting your writing Preparing an outline • Writing your piece Style • Summary

Efficient proof reading

When in doubt throw it out: Personal organisation quiz

Keep a clear desk

Dejunk your desk

Fantastic filing

The ten commandments of e-mail: Some golden rules

Improve note taking with mind maps: Why use mind maps? • Drawing basic mind maps • Improving your mind maps • Summary

Active reading: Read quicker and more effectively

Knowing what you want to know: Knowing how deeply to study the material • Speed reading magazines and

seven

When in doubt – throw it out

Except for filing cabinets and your desk, remove from your office any item on which you accumulate paperwork. It will force you to make decisions on a timely basis.

There is little doubt that we are drowning in paperwork. Whether it is mail-shots, memos, magazines, reports or letters, there is a constant avalanche of this material falling onto our desks every single day. Despite computer networks and electronic mail, we seem to be creating more paper not less. So much for the paperless office.

Most people's approach to this paperwork avalanche is this, 'Keep everything and just decide what to throw away.' However, this is not effective as we end up with piles and piles of information everywhere. The sensible approach, and perhaps the only sustainable way to manage paperwork is this, 'Throw everything away, except for a few things that you need to keep.'

We can successfully apply the 80/20 rule to our paperwork. Eighty per cent of paperwork that crosses our desk to gain our attention is probably trivial or at best useful for a very short period of time. Twenty per cent will be more important and may need to be referred to or actioned later. This is the 20 per cent which we should keep. Simply throwing more away can be the leap-frog into the more successful management of information and paperwork.

Get yourself off unnecessary mailing lists – just send back junk mail unopened – don't bin it – they will probably send more.

The average employed person can spend up to 45 minutes per day looking for things. Now of course this may not be just paperwork, it might be books, keys, computer files and so on, but probably these things are buried under piles of paper.

Personal organisation quiz

		Yes	No
1.	Do you sometimes worry about losing important pieces of paper – receipts, invoices, letters, statements?		
2.	Do you sometimes have a pile of things you never get round to reading?		
3.	Do you sometimes miss call-backs or appointments because your diary system has let you down?		
4.	Is your desk as you left it last night?		
5.	Do you have paperwork on your desk which is more than three weeks old?		
6.	Do you have things on your desk which are only there because you do not know what to do with them?		
7.	Do you sometimes buy things which you do not need, with money you don't really have, to impress people you don't really like?		
8.	If you found your ideal home, perfect in every detail, except that it did not have enough storage space, would you buy it?		
9.	If you had a drop-in visitor in your office or home would you be embarrassed by the way they found the place?		
10.	Could you direct somebody to a piece of paper on your desk over the 'phone from this room? Not by saying 'It's in that pile by the telephone, if it's not in there try the pile on the floor.' I mean precisely.		
11.	When you open high cupboards do you fear for your life?		
12.	Do you have more than one To-do list?		
13.	Do you sometimes find yourself either at work or home having trouble throwing things away?		

If you have answered 'Yes' to six or more questions then you are what might be called 'organisationally challenged.' If you have more then nine you could be described as 'debris dysfunctional.'

Avoid clutter. Keep everything you are not working on out of your immediate working area and out of sight, if possible. Always tidy up your desk and work area before leaving the office.

Keep a clear desk

After prioritisation, aim to pick up a piece of paper only if you mean to finish working with it then. Don't be a paper shuffler.

In most cases, a clear desk is a signal and a trait of someone who is organised, professional and effective. There are numerous benefits for keeping a clear desk, here are just a few:

1. It is more motivating when you come into work in the morning.
2. It stops or prevents people putting things on your desk – people often hesitate to put things on top of a clear desk and would rather put it in a tray or will wait to give it to you.
3. You lose things less frequently.
4. You are less likely to be distracted by pieces of paper, files or reports that catch the corner of your eye when you are working on something else.
5. You are less likely to spill coffee or drinks.
6. You are less likely to lose important messages or post-it notes. (I have missed whole meetings, because somebody kept a post-it note on their desk which got buried and forgot to tell me the message.)
7. It gives clear signals to people that you are organised and you use your time well.
8. It creates a sense of efficiency and an air of authority in an office.

Here is a step-by-step process that will help you achieve this clear desk.

Use a 'slush' file or have a specific place to put all papers which are not important enough to file permanently, but which you currently feel uncomfortable about throwing away.

Dejunk your desk

1. Think about how often you use different objects and store them accordingly. Keep the desktop free for in-trays containing urgent paperwork, a pot of pens and the phone, with a list of most-used numbers and a book for messages to yourself.
2. Once a week sort the paper on your desk into four piles: act on, bin, file, and pass on. It shouldn't take you more than a few seconds to make each decision.
3. Review your filing system. Keep files lean and bin anything that is duplicated before you put it away.
4. Take ten minutes every morning to organise your day. Make a list of priorities and tackle the most challenging tasks first. Mornings are your most creative time. Clear your desk then.
5. Get grievances with colleagues sorted or make a decision to forget them, and stop shuffling issues or writing memos/ e-mails.
6. Avoid having loose paper on the desktop or in filing trays – use plastic or card files. It makes things easier to find, keeps paper together and looks good!

Sort your post/ paperwork standing-up... not at your desk. This avoids the temptation to put it back down on the desk.

Fantastic filing

Whenever you touch a piece of paper you have to do something with it. Try this, any time you touch or read a piece of correspondence put a dot in the corner...

Here are a few basic principles:

1. Filing systems only measure how quickly you can find information, the less paper stored, the faster you can find things.
2. Purge the filing system every three months. Throw away anything you don't need. Information dates quickly.
3. The things immediately around you in the office should only be for the current 12 months. Archive everything else. You may need to find it occasionally but usually you do not need it – you may need to keep it for legal reasons.
4. Be alert to *Parkinson's Law of Filing Cabinets*. Paperwork expands to fill the space available. Never buy your staff extra cabinets because they do not have enough space. They will fill it and ask for another six months later.
5. *Parkinson's Law of Briefcases*. Paperwork expands to fill the case. Do you buy a bigger briefcase as the one you have does not hold enough? You then buy another bigger one or two etc. Keep a lean, mean and smart filing system.
6. Learn to pass it on, give it to somebody else.
7. Dump it. Most people attach a pile of paper with the 'mind set' that they will keep most and throw a little away. Eighty per cent kept, 20 per cent thrown. Reverse it. Throw away 80 per cent and just keep 20 per cent.
8. You may need to have things to hand. Keep them in files. Keep them in those clear view wallets. Keep them together.
9. Do not let loose paper roam round the desk. Keep a whole file, one per project, per person.

...if it looks like a case of measles by the end of the week, do something with it. Phone the person, write to them, action it, file it. The filing system you use will vary according to your job.

10. Keep a file for each of the people you need to deal with regularly. Every time something comes in for one of them put it in the file and give them the information when you see them.

Set up a desk data file (sometimes called a future file, a suspense file or tickler file) to provide an automatic method of bringing papers to your attention on specific dates in the future.

The ten commandments of e-mail

Learn to touch type, until speech input or cerebral-downloading catches on, it will save you hours.

It is possible to send e-mail shots to thousands of people with a single key stroke. By setting up user-groups with an organisation I can CC anybody and everybody with no extra effort. Paper communication (snail mail) would require photo-copying and envelope stuffing and perhaps posting. The trouble with e-mail is that it is too easy.

It is not uncommon for people to receive 50-100 e-mails a day. In some organisations it has been claimed to be a major source of stress and sometimes people may spend two hours just reading and sending e-mails!

Some golden rules

1. Use the 80/20 rule to scan and select which e-mails to read first.
2. Adopt a simple code system for internal e-mails – IO – Information Only, AR – Action Required, RD – Read and Destroy.
3. Don't become an e-mail junkie – pick up your e-mail at set intervals or times. Turn off the e-mail alert signal on your computer.
4. If the header doesn't make the e-mail sound interesting or relevant – don't read; delete it unread. If the sender can't make it sound worth reading that is their problem not yours! The chances are that it is not worth reading anyway.

5. Limit how long you spend reading e-mails.
6. Send CC copies that are not your concern back unread.
7. Keep your e-mail to short, informal, punchy, lists. Headings and bullet points are important.
8. Read the first and last paragraph of an e-mail first – the middle is probably waffle.
9. Don't keep e-mails on your computer – delete them when read – the sender will always have a copy if you need it.
10. Don't print and file a copy – this is pointless and defeats the purpose of e-mail

Do not copy people that don't **NEED** to know, this sets a precedent and they then add you to their CC list.

Have two or three e-mail boxes – perhaps one for general e-mail which you glance at, one for customers or priority contacts and one for close staff or colleagues. This will make it easier to differentiate between 'need to know' and 'nice to know'.

Improve note taking with mind maps

Mind Mapping is a very important technique for noting information. Mind Maps have been developed and popularised by Tony Buzan.

Why use mind maps?

Mind Maps abandon the list structure of conventional note taking in favour of a two dimensional structure. A good Mind Map shows the 'shape' of the subject, the relative importance of information and ideas, and the way that information relates to other information.

Typically Mind Maps are more compact than conventional notes, often taking up one side of paper. This helps associations to be made easily. Information that is acquired after the main Mind Map has been drawn can easily be integrated with minimal disruption. Mind Maps can be used to summarise and consolidate information from different research sources, to think through complex problems and they are a way of presenting information that shows the overall structure of your subject.

Mind Maps are also very quick to review – it is easy to refresh information in your mind just before it is needed by glancing at one. For people who have spatial memories, Mind Maps can provide effective mnemonics – remembering the shape and structure of a Mind Map can provide the cues necessary to remember the information contained within them. Mind Maps engage much more of the brain in the process of assimilating and connecting facts than conventional notes.

Drawing basic mind maps

A basic Mind Map is drawn in the following way:

1. Write the title of the subject in the centre of the page, and draw a circle around it.
2. For the first main heading of the subject, draw a line out from the circle in any direction, and write the heading above or below the line.
3. For sub-headings of the main heading, draw lines out from the first line for each sub-heading and label each one.
4. For individual facts, draw lines out from the appropriate heading line.

A complete Mind Map may have main topic lines radiating in all directions, with sub-topics and facts branching off from these, like branches and twigs from the trunk of a tree. Do not worry about the structure produced – this will evolve of its own accord.

Improving your mind maps

Your Mind Maps are your own property. Once you understand how to assemble the basic structure, you can develop your own coding and conventions to take things further, for example to show linkages between facts. The following suggestions, however, may help to enhance the effectiveness of your Mind Maps:

Use single words or simple phrases for information

The majority of words in normal texts are padding – they ensure that facts are conveyed in the correct context to another person in a format that is pleasant to read. In your own Mind Maps, single strong words and evocative phrases can convey the same meaning. Excess words just clutter the Mind Map, and take time to write down.

Print words

Indistinct writing can be more difficult to read and less attractive to look at. Use colour to separate different ideas: this will help your mind to separate ideas where that is necessary, and helps visualisation of the Mind Map for recall. Colour also helps to show organisation.

Use of symbols and images

Where a symbol means something to you, and conveys more information than words, use it. Pictures will help you to remember information.

Use shapes, circles and boundaries to connect information

These are additional tools to help show the grouping of information.

Use arrows

To show the cause and effect.

Summary

Mind Maps provide an extremely effective method of taking notes which shows the structure of a subject and the relative importance of facts and ideas in addition to the facts themselves. Mind Maps help to associate ideas and make connections that would otherwise be too unrelated to be linked. If you do any form of research or note-taking, try experimenting with Mind Maps. You will be surprised by their effectiveness.

Active reading

Read quicker and more effectively

When we are young we are taught to read to a level of basic competence. Unfortunately teaching stops before moving on to the advanced skills which can significantly increase the speed at which we read.

There are two main approaches to improving reading skills: speed reading, which increases the number of words that can be read in a minute, and use of reading strategies to extract information from a text in the most effective way possible. Speed reading is covered elsewhere. This section will concentrate on effective use of reading strategies and will cover the following:

- Active reading
- Knowing what you want to know
- Knowing how deeply to study the text
- Knowing how to read different sorts of material
- Reading newspapers and magazines
- Article types
- Reading junk mail
- Reading technical information
- Reading reports

In handling correspondence, consider answering routine letters and memos on the original, photocopying them for your own records and returning the original to the sender.

When you read it is useful to highlight, underline and annotate the text as you go. This emphasises information in your mind, and helps you to review important points after you have finished studying the text.

Active reading helps to keep your mind focused on the material and stops it wandering.

This is obviously only something to do if you own the document! If you find that active reading helps significantly, then it may be worth photocopying information in more expensive texts. You can then read and mark the photocopies.

Knowing what you want to know

The most important thing to know is the goal of your study – what do you want to know after reading the text? Once you know this you can examine the text to see whether it is going to move you towards the goal.

An easy way of doing this is to look at the introduction and the chapter headings. The introduction should let you know who the book is targeted at and what it seeks to achieve, while the chapter headings will give an overall view of the structure of the subject.

While you are looking at the text, ask yourself if it is targeted at you, or assumes too much or too little knowledge. Would other material meet your needs more closely?

Knowing how deeply to study the material

Where you only need the shallowest knowledge of the subject, skim the material – read only chapter headings, introductions and summaries.

If you need a moderate level of information on a subject, then you can scan the text. Here you read the chapter introductions and summaries in detail, and speed-read the contents of the chapters, picking out and understanding key words and concepts.

Learn to read routine material more rapidly. Do not 'backtrack,' compulsively rereading phrases before going on.

At this level of looking at the document it is worth paying attention to diagrams and graphs.

Only when you need detailed knowledge of a subject is it worth studying the text – skim the material first to get an overview of the subject. Once you have done this you can read it in detail while seeing how the information presented relates to the overall structure of the subject. An effective method of getting the deepest level of understanding possible from a text is to use a formal method such as SQ3R (see page 158).

Speed reading magazines and newspapers

These tend to give a very fragmented coverage of a subject, concentrating on the most interesting and glamorous parts of a topic while ignoring the less interesting but often essential background. Typically areas of useful information are padded out with large areas of irrelevant data or with advertising.

The most effective way of dealing with magazines is to scan their contents tables or indexes, turning directly to interesting articles. If the articles are useful they can be cut out and filed into a folder specifically covering that sort of information. The magazine can then be binned. In this way you build up sets of related articles. Information can then be retrieved easily and quickly.

Newspapers tend to be arranged in sections. If you read a paper frequently you can learn which sections have useful information, and which ones can be skipped.

By applying an intelligent way of reading newspapers and magazines you can significantly speed the time it takes to extract the information you need from them.

Article types and how to read them

Articles within newspapers and magazines tend to be in three main types:

News articles

The most important information is presented first, with information being less and less significant as the article progresses. News articles are designed to explain the key points first, and then flesh them out with detail.

> Use window envelopes where appropriate for correspondence, saving the time of a second typing of the name and address.

Opinion articles

These are designed to advance a viewpoint. Here the most important information is contained in the introduction and the summary, with the middle of the article containing supporting arguments.

Feature articles

These are written to provide entertainment or background on a subject. Typically the most important information is in the body of the text.

If you know what you want from an article, and recognise its type, you can extract information from it quickly and efficiently.

Deal with mail effectively

Dealing with junk mail can take up a significant amount of time.

A useful technique is to touch each document only once; either act on it, bin it or file it. Effectively written direct mail will convey its purpose immediately, and will assist you in extracting and acting on information rapidly. Badly written direct mail is tedious and can take a lot of time to digest. Bin it immediately.

When you decide to act on direct mail, it is best to do so by phone, fax or e-mail, rather than by writing a formal letter.

Read technical information effectively

Technical information is typically less friendly than other information. It is often complex and assumes a high level of initial knowledge.

Manuals are often badly written – a manual is often supplied with a product purely because it is expected. In some cases it will have been given to a junior member of staff to prepare and will not have been properly edited or reviewed.

Before wading into technical documentation, assess who it has been written for. Is it too basic or too advanced? In the latter case it may be more cost effective to bring in an expert to do the job.

If referring to specific information, it is most effective to use the table of contents and index to find the appropriate section.

If you are reading large amounts of the material, it may be effective to photocopy the glossary, and keep this beside you. It may also be useful to note down the key concepts in your own words, and refer to them when necessary. Usually the most effective way of making notes is to use Mind Maps (see page 146). As with other sorts of material it may be most effective to skim the material before reading it in depth.

Reading 'whole subject' documents

When you are reading a document, such as a company report, which purports to give an overall analysis of a subject, it is easy to accept the writer's structure of thought, and miss the fact that important information has been omitted or that irrelevant detail has been included.

Where you are reviewing this sort of document, an effective technique is to compile your own table of contents headings before you start. You can then use this table of contents to read the document in the order that you want.

This technique will allow you to spot where important information is missing or has been obscured, and helps you to avoid trivia. If the writer has a better knowledge of the structure of the topic, this helps you to recognise and adjust your initial view of the best structure.

Improving reading speed

Improvement of reading rate

It is safe to say that almost anyone can double their speed of reading while maintaining equal or even higher comprehension.

The average college student reads between 250 and 350 words per minute on fiction and non-technical materials. A 'good' reading speed is around 500 to 700 words per minute, but some people can read a thousand words per minute or even faster on these materials. What makes the difference? There are three main factors involved in improving reading speed:

1. The desire to improve
2. The willingness to try new techniques
3. The motivation to practice.

The role of speed in the reading process

Understanding the role of speed in the reading process is essential. Research has shown a close relation between speed and understanding. For example, in checking progress charts of thousands of individuals taking reading training, it has been found in most cases that an increase in rate has been paralleled by an increase in comprehension, and that where rate has gone down, comprehension has also decreased.

Although there is at present little statistical evidence, it seems that plodding word-by-word analysation (or word reading) inhibits understanding. There is some reason to believe that the factors producing slow reading are also involved in lowered comprehension. Most adults are able to increase their rate of reading considerably and rather quickly without lowering comprehension. These same individuals seldom show an increase in comprehension when they reduce their rate. In other cases, comprehension is actually better at higher rates of speed. Such results, of course, are heavily dependent upon the method used to gain the increased rate. Simply reading more rapidly without actual improvement in basic reading habits usually results in lowered comprehension.

Basic conditions for increased reading rate

A well planned programme prepares for maximum increase in rate by establishing the necessary conditions. Five basic conditions include:

1. Have your eyes checked – very slow reading is often related to uncorrected eye defects.
2. Eliminate the habit of pronouncing words as you read. You should be able to read most materials at least two or three times faster silently than orally. If you are aware of sounding or 'hearing' words as you read, try to concentrate on key words and meaningful ideas as you force yourself to read faster.
3. Avoid regressing (rereading). The average student reading at 250 words per minute regresses or rereads about 20 times per page. Usually, it is unnecessary to reread words, for the ideas you want are explained and elaborated more fully in later contexts.
4. Furthermore, the slowest reader usually regresses most frequently. Because he reads slowly, his mind has time to wander and his rereading reflects both his inability to concentrate and his lack of confidence in his comprehension skills.
5. Develop a wider eye-span. This will help you to read more than one word at a glance. Since written material is less meaningful if read word by word, this will help you to learn to read by phrases or thought units.

Rate adjustment

Poor results are inevitable if the reader attempts to use the same rate indiscriminately for a-1 (important and urgent material) types of material and for all other reading purposes. He must learn to adjust his rate to his purpose in reading and to the difficulty of the material being read. This ranges from a maximum rate on easy, familiar, interesting material to a minimal rate on material which is unfamiliar in content and language structure or which must be thoroughly digested. The effective reader adjusts his rate; the ineffective reader uses the same rate for all types of material.

Rate adjustment may be overall adjustment to the article as a whole, or internal adjustment within the article. Overall adjustment establishes the basic rate at which the total article is read; internal adjustment involves the necessary variations in rate for each varied part of the material. As an analogy, you plan to take a 100-mile mountain trip. Since this will be a relatively hard drive with hills, curves, and a mountain pass, you decide to take three hours for the total trip, averaging about 35 miles an hour. This is your overall rate adjustment. However, in actual driving you may slow down to no more than 15 miles per hour on some curves and hills, while speeding up to 50 miles per hour or more on relatively straight and level sections. This is your internal rate adjustment. There is no set rate, therefore, which the good reader follows inflexibly in reading a particular selection, even though he has set himself an overall rate for the total job.

Overall rate adjustment should be based on your reading plan, your reading purpose, and the nature and difficulty of the material. The reading plan itself should specify the general rate to be used. This is based on the total 'size up'. It may be helpful to consider examples of how purpose can act to help determine the rate to be used. *To understand information, skim or scan at a rapid rate.*

To determine the value of material or to read for enjoyment, read rapidly or slowly according to your feeling. To read analytically, read at a moderate pace to permit interrelating ideas. The nature and difficulty of the material requires an adjustment in rate in conformity with your ability to handle that type of material. Obviously, the level of difficulty is highly relative to the particular reader. Generally, difficult material will entail a slower rate; simpler material will permit a faster rate.

Internal rate adjustment involves selecting differing rates for parts of a given article. In general, decrease speed when you find the following:

- Unfamiliar terminology not clear in context. Try to understand it in context at that point; otherwise, read on and return to it later.
- Difficult sentence and paragraph structure; slow down enough to enable you to untangle them and get accurate context for the passage.
- Unfamiliar or abstract concepts. Look for applications or examples of your own as well as studying those of the writer. Take enough time to get them clearly in mind.
- Detailed, technical material. This includes complicated directions, statements of difficult principles, materials on which you have scant background.
- Material on which you want detailed retention. In general, increase speed when you meet the following:
    - simple material with few ideas which are new to you; move rapidly over the familiar ones; spend most of your time on the unfamiliar ideas
    - unnecessary examples and illustrations. Since these are included to clarify ideas, move over them rapidly when they are not needed
    - detailed explanation and idea elaboration which you do not need
    - broad, generalised ideas and ideas which are restatements of previous ones. These can be readily grasped, even with scan techniques.

In keeping your reading attack flexible, adjust your rate sensitivity from article to article. It is equally important to adjust your rate within a given article. Practice these techniques until a flexible reading rate becomes second nature to you.

Summary

In summary, evidence has been cited which seems to indicate a need for and value of a rapid rate of reading, while at the same time indicating the dangers of speed in reading. We have attempted to point out the relationship between rate of reading and extent of comprehension, as well as the necessity for adjustment of reading rate, along with whole reading attack, to the type of material and the purposes of the reader.

SQ3R: Survey, Question, Read, Recall and Review

SQ3R is a technique used to learn from a document by firstly understanding it, and then building a mental framework into which facts can be fitted. SQ3R stands for the stages in which information can be assimilated:

- Survey
- Question
- Read
- Recall
- Review

Survey

Survey the document: scan the contents, introduction, chapter introductions and chapter summaries to pick up a shallow overview of the text and form an opinion of whether it will be of any help.

Question

Make a note of any questions which result from your initial survey. Perhaps rescan the document to see if any questions stand out. These questions can be considered almost as study goals – understanding the answers can help you to structure the information in your own mind.

Read

Now read the document. Read through it in detail, taking care to understand all the points that are relevant. In the case of some texts this reading may be very slow if there is a lot of dense and complicated information.

Recall

Once you have read the document, or a section of it, run through it in your mind a number of times. Isolate the core facts or the essential processes behind the subject, and then see how other information fits around them. Some things may require more recital than others for them to sink in.

Review

Once you have run through the exercise of recalling the information, you can move on to the stage of reviewing the information. This review can be by re-reading the document, by expanding your notes, or by discussing the material with someone else. A particularly effective method of reviewing information is to have to teach it to someone else!

Communicate information quickly and effectively

Targeting your writing

It is essential to have a clear idea of who your reader is. You should know why he or she is going to be reading your piece, where and when they will be reading it, and what they will want to get out of it.

Knowing this, and knowing what information you want to convey allows you to decide an aim for the article. You should focus on content, structure, style and presentation.

Preparing an outline

Once you have decided the aim of the article, you are ready to prepare an outline. This allows you to start to organise the information into a coherent structure. If you start writing without an outline you are in danger of producing a disorganised, chaotic mess that confuses your reader and fails to make the desired connections in his or her mind.

If you have researched the article by using a Mind Map or by noting conventionally, an effective way of producing an outline is to open up a word processor document and to type in the facts that you have decided to include. You can then cut and paste these notes into related groups, and order these groups in a way that supports your argument.

Once you have selected information and organised a structure, prepare an outline of the introduction and summary. The shape of these should be obvious from the structure you have given your information. The introduction should help the reader to prepare an overall structure into which the information in the article can be fitted. The summary should organise the facts in the middle of the article into a coherent whole.

Writing your piece

When you have prepared your outline, it is time to start writing!

The easiest way of doing this is to just let the words and ideas flow. Move quickly through the piece without editing or reviewing it. This will help to keep your creativity flowing without it being crippled by self-criticism.

Only when you have finished a section should you review it. At this stage you may decide to reorganise it, edit it, change it around, and add or delete information. As you review it you should check that what you have written meets the aim you set and gives the reader the information they want.

Style

The style of the article should be completely focused on the reader's needs. Language used should be pitched at the appropriate level for the reader.

People generally prefer information presented in short sentences with little or no jargon. You may be tempted to write in a way that you think will impress your readers, using long words and complex sentences. All this shows is that you are not able to communicate ideas clearly and simply. It is likely that material written like this will not be read at all.

If you need to use technical language that may not be understood, include a glossary.

Remember that you have responsibility for the clarity, effectiveness and focus of your communication. Beyond this, style will emerge on its own without you needing to worry about it.

Summary

1. Know who you are writing for, and what they will want from your writing.
2. Prepare an outline to give structure to your piece.
3. Include an introduction and summary to help readers to structure information in their minds.
4. When you write, try to let words and ideas flow.
5. Only edit and review a section once you have completed its first draft.
6. As you review it, ensure that the material meets the aim you set for the piece.

The style of the piece should be focused on the readers' needs. Avoid trying to impress people with your knowledge. Remember that the responsibility for effective communication lies with you!

Efficient proof-reading

Proof-reading is not an innate ability; it is an acquired skill. The following exercises will help you master it, or at any rate will impress you with how difficult it is.

Hints for successful proof-reading

1. Cultivate a healthy sense of doubt.
2. If there are certain types of errors you know you tend to make, double check for those.
3. Read very slowly.
4. If possible, read out loud.
5. Read one word at a time.
6. Read what is actually on the page, not what you think is there (this is the most difficult sub-skill to acquire, particularly if you wrote what you are reading).
7. If possible, work with someone else.

Most errors in written work are made unconsciously. There are two sources of unconscious error:

1. **Faculty information from the kinaesthetic memory. If you have always misspelled a word like 'accommodate', you will unthinkingly misspell it again.**
2. **A split second of inattention. The mind works far faster than the pen or keyboard.**

It is the unconscious nature of the errors that makes proof-reading so difficult. The person who turned in a paper saying, 'I like girdle cakes for breakfast' did not have a perverted digestion. He thought he had written 'griddle cakes' and because that's what he was sure he had written, that's what he 'saw' when he proof-read. If he had slowed down and read word by word, out loud, he might have caught the error. You have to doubt every word in order to catch every mistake.

Another reason for deliberately slowing down is that when you read normally, you often see only the shells of words – the first and last few letters, perhaps. You 'fix your eyes' on the print only three or four times (or less) per line. You take in the words between your fixation points with your peripheral vision, which gets less accurate the farther it is from the point. The average reader can only take in six letters accurately with one fixation. This means you have to fix your eyes on almost every word you have written and do it twice for longer words, in order to proof-read accurately. You have to look at the word, not slide over it.

In proof-reading, you can take nothing for granted, because unconscious mistakes are so easy to make. It helps to read out loud, because you are forced to slow down and you hear what you are reading as well as seeing it, so you are using two senses. It is often possible to hear a mistake, such as an omitted or repeated word that you have not seen.

Professional editors proof-read as many as ten times. Publishing houses hire teams of readers to work in pairs, out loud. And still errors occur.

Remember that it is twice as hard to detect mistakes in your own work as in someone elses!

Overcoming procrastination

Why do we resist change? Action diversions • Emotional diversions • Mental diversions

How to stop procrastination: Action change steps • Emotional change steps • Mental change steps • Conclusion • Overcoming procrastination

Techniques to manage procrastination

Seven day procrastination plan

Procrastination: Ten ways to 'do it now': Remedies • Do it now!

eight

Why do we resist change?

Procrastination often occurs when we are required to change. Rearranging the office, starting a diet, giving up smoking, all become tomorrow's activities. Feeling a lack of accomplishment, surrounded by incomplete projects, losing opportunities, experiencing many unpleasant emotional consequences, and feeling irresponsible, why don't procrastinators just act effectively and rid themselves of these unwanted outcomes?

The explanation is this: we are complex, inventive creatures who do not always act in our enlightened self-interest. We can, and do, distract ourselves from our problems and reconstruct them to make them temporarily more digestible. When it comes to procrastination, we normally live in a twilight zone and avoid changes when it comes to our cherished procrastination-evoking assumptions and beliefs. Here are some action, emotional and mental distractions which support procrastination patterns that you can watch for and change.

Schedule nasty jobs for specific times and reward yourself on completion.

Action diversions

Action diversions involve substituting a low priority activity for legitimate maintenance or developmental work.

Emotional diversions

People who fall into the emotional diversion trap wait for the moment of inspiration to strike where they 'feel right'- ie can happily and effortlessly deal with their outstanding projects. You don't have to feel inspired to get things done, however, how many of us feel inspired to scrub a dirty floor or face a difficult confrontation? Although some complex challenges may require time to think out and to 'work up' to a solution, most activities can either be started or accomplished in the present.

Mental diversions

Set a time limit and do it then!

Procrastinators often play a variety of mental tricks on themselves. One trick is the mañana ploy, where you think tomorrow it is going to be easier to do what you feel like putting off today. When tomorrow comes, the project keeps getting put off to a later time until it turns into a crisis. The contingency mañana ploy is a bit more sophisticated. Here you make one action depend on the completion of another, then you put off the preliminary activity: eg you think you need to do research about losing weight before you start to develop new eating habits.

The Catch-22 ploy is even more pernicious. Here you quit before you begin because you have created an impossible condition for yourself. You declare that you need an MBA to have the career you secretly desire, then you declare yourself to be not intelligent enough to obtain this degree. Result: you don't take the steps to improve and feel frustrated with what you do. Finally, the backward ploy is one where you dwell on real or perceived mistakes from the past. This is a variation on the Catch-22 ploy: you believe you can't go forward unless you can change what has already happened. Since you can't change the past, no amount of mental rehashing will help.

Although recognising how these diversions work won't automatically reverse your procrastination, a rational awareness of what is going on means that you can start to change your thinking, emotions, and actions by following some of the basic strategies listed overleaf.

How to stop procrastination

To varying degrees, most of us can learn to replace many of the unpleasant consequences of procrastination with the results of accomplishment. Although this takes effort and persistence, our self-improvement actions can lead to what Stanford University professor Albert Bandura calls *self-efficacy*. This is a fact-based belief that you can exercise control over events that affect your life. This constructive belief motivates and regulates the actions that you take. To change from a pattern of procrastination to a process of self-efficacy may involve many false starts, advances, relapses, and backsliding. Change rarely follows an uninterrupted course!

Action change steps

Start with clear, measurable, achievable goals. It is better to say you are going to work on your income taxes two hours each Saturday morning for the month of February, than to say you are going to stop procrastinating on your taxes.

Take a 'bits and pieces' approach. Even the most complex of tasks have simple beginnings. Break the activity down so you can tackle each phase with a reasonable expectation of progress. This method may be particularly useful for projects such as writing assignments, career development or building self-efficacy.

Use the five minute method. Begin by committing five minutes to get started, then do it! In that five minute period, do something to finish the project; then you decide if you are going to continue for another five minutes. Follow this pattern until you decide to quit, or are done. If you decide to quit before you are done, take five minutes to set up what you will do to get a jump on the task when next you begin. Through this method you only commit to short work periods. This can be a surprisingly effective way to break your inertia. There are many ways to get organised and set the stage for follow-through actions. Here is a simple way to organise your work to overcome procrastination. Set up a **catch-up**, **keep-up** and **get-ahead** filing system. Make a current activity list for each file, and modify the lists as you progress. The catch-up file includes long-overdue activities that you want to finish. Set aside time each day to work on the items in this file, checking the tasks off as you get them done. In your keep-up file, emphasise getting priority matters done as they come up. These are the activities that could otherwise become problems later on or lead to lost opportunities. For your get-ahead file, schedule time blocks to initiate steps to advance your personal interests. Get-ahead file time can involve planning or acting.

The activities lists contained in all three files may vary as your life demands and priorities vary. Although unexpected interruptions may temporarily distract you, over a six-month period this programme can yield the following benefits:

- You have no more catch-up file
- You manage your keep-up projects with a reasonable amount of effectiveness
- You spend significant time on your get-ahead projects, and
- You experience a sound sense of accomplishment and advantage. (Note: You can list and then check off your gains in each of the three groups. This check-off strategy can give you a visual reward for your efforts.)

When you feel tempted to substitute a low priority activity (reading a tabloid or watching a soap opera) for a priority project, make the substitute activities contingent on doing part or all of the priority activity first. Here the 'substitute' activity can serve as a reward that immediately follows a catch-up, keep-up, or get-ahead action.

Complete spontaneously occurring tasks as they arise: **DO IT NOW**.

Emotional change steps

Can you imagine changing frustration avoidance into frustration challenging?

When you experience mild levels of tension that you normally associate with activity avoidance, concentrate on this tension. Note where the tension is located. Is it in your shoulders, stomach, or mind? Acknowledging, accepting, and exploring a strained feeling can sometimes make it more tolerable. Now, try to use your tension as a catalyst for a counter-procrastination action.

By setting up lofty, unrealistic, and perfectionist standards you can depress yourself by defining yourself as powerless to achieve the standard. Try shifting your attention from this depressive flow of thought by using a brief one minute relaxation breathing exercise:

- Take about five seconds to gradually fill your lungs with air.
- Hold your breath for five seconds.
- Breathe out slowly and evenly until you have expelled the air from your lungs.
- Wait five seconds before breathing in. Repeat the pattern three more times, then breathe normally. Now, act – whether you feel relaxed or not!

Although most people dislike doing things when they feel uncomfortable or uncertain about an outcome, consider whether this tension would prevent you from acting if somebody offered you a million dollars to do the task. If that causes a shift in your perspective, act on that new perspective without the reward. If you experience no new shift in perspective, switch to the five-minute plan.

Recall a time when you felt motivated and effective. Think about the sights, scents, sounds, and emotions you experienced. Use this recollection as a catalyst to act. If you can't reconstruct a motivating experience, do something to start the put-off project: motivation often follows action.

Mental change steps

Listen for anxiety-creating self-talk when you start to procrastinate. Challenge these thoughts by pushing yourself into problem solving actions.

Listen for self-downing self-talk. Confront this negative self-talk by evoking an action perspective on the challenge you face. Here is how: consider that, as a complex human being, you have thousands of accomplishments. Next, consider that you have about 18,000 different personal attributes and qualities. Some of your capabilities will be stronger than others. List those capabilities that have either led to accomplishment or that you believe you can develop. Exercise them and watch them grow.

Deal with anxious or depressed thoughts as they arise. Both anxiety and depression share a common overly generalised belief; 'I'm powerless because I can't cope.' To help yourself break this procrastination catalyst, first reverse this statement to see the circularity ('I can't cope because I'm powerless.') Next, recognise that the generalised circular idea is a belief, not a fact. Then ask yourself 'What are the exceptions to this belief?' Honest answers to this question can start you toward a fresh new perspective, reasonably free of the type of overgeneralised circular reasoning that is often at the core of human disturbance and procrastination.

Conclusion

Procrastination patterns are not trivial matters. Practically every form of procrastination eventually leads to disadvantages of various types and degrees. When you actively select and respond to important challenges, you will add to your chances of improving yourself.

Procrastination is not a simple act of putting something off. This process has more twists than might first appear. It is a symptom of self-doubt, self-downing, discomfort-dodging and irrational guilt. The results of procrastination can be a stimulus for the faulty beliefs that evoked procrastination in the first place. It can be a defence against fear of failure, and, therefore, serve as a diversion from facing that fear. It can be a well-practised problem habit.

To complicate this already twisted mental labyrinth, you embrace many diversionary strategies that obscure your primary reasons for procrastinating. It is hard to catch yourself in the act of procrastinating while engaged in diversionary pursuits.

How to make decisions fast: decide on **two** choices or decisions and label each **heads** or **tails.** Tell yourself you will do which side of the coin lands face up when you toss it. Toss the coin. You will know the right decision to make when the coin lands.

Overcoming procrastination

Face and overcome procrastination by first committing yourself to work toward achievable goals. These are goals where you articulate the meaning of what you want to accomplish and do so in measurable terms. The goal 'I want to be happy' is a false goal, because happiness is a by-product of doing something else first. It doesn't qualify as a legitimate goal for this exercise. Working three consecutive hours on planning a get-ahead strategy is concrete, measurable, and thus attainable.

Recognise that the change process is rarely smooth. Situations will vary as will your ability to concentrate and respond. If you are like most people, you'll have your peaks and valleys.

Persist at becoming more efficient and effective and improve the quality of your life.

Techniques to manage procrastination

A lot of stress in peoples' lives revolves around time. Procrastination is probably the number one time management problem of all! The causes of procrastination are as numerous and varied as the excuses we invent for them. Procrastination can be an effective mask for our own unrealistic perfectionist tendencies, self-doubt or fear of change, or it can simply be a result of poor time management and ineffective study skills.

Here are some tips to help you live with your procrastination and still be able to get your work done and enjoy life:

- Accept procrastination as a normal human behaviour.
- Be realistic – only prioritise a couple of tasks or goals each day.
- Create a schedule that allows for unanticipated events – such as computer crashes, mistakes and distractions.
- Forgive yourself if you don't complete all the tasks on your list of things to do.
- Choose a level that is 'good-enough' for each task. Every project that you do doesn't need to be perfect.
- Give yourself a break and schedule time for play! Play renews your energy so that your work habits are more effective.
- Warn your friends and loved ones that you'll be unavailable and unbearable the last few hours (or days) during those times when you're going to procrastinate and end up cramming anyway!

Set priorities

- **Not**: I don't know where to begin, so I can't begin at all.
- **Instead**: The most important step is to pick one project to focus on.

Break the task down into little pieces

- **Not**: There's so much to do, and it's so complicated.
- **Instead**: I don't have to do the whole project at once. There are separate small steps I can take.

Set up small, specific goals

- **Not**: I have to write my thesis within two months.
- **Instead**: If I write two pages per day, Monday – Friday, I can finish a first draft in a month. I'll have a revised final draft in two months.

Take one small step at a time

- **Not**: It's too much. I'll never get it all done.
- **Instead**: What is the next step on my list? I'll concentrate on that step for right now.

Reward yourself right away when you accomplish a small goal

- **Not**: I can't take any time out until I'm completely finished.
- **Instead**: I spent an hour working. Now I'll call a friend.

Use a time schedule

- **Not**: I must devote the whole week to this project.
- **Instead**: I can use these times this week to work on my project: Monday 7-8; Tuesday 7-9; Saturday 10-12.

Learn how to tell the time

- **Not**: Sorting through these papers and reorganising my file cabinet will be a snap. It won't take me more than an hour, so I can do it any time.
- **Instead**: Sorting papers always takes longer than I expect, so I'll start tonight. I'll spend one hour filing a stack of papers.

Optimise your chances for success

- **Not**: I'll do my writing this weekend at home.
- **Instead**: I'll write during the week in a library – this is a good place to get my work done.

Delegate, where possible

- **Not**: I am the only person in the world who can do this.

- **Instead**: I don't have to do this all by myself. I can ask someone else to do part of the job and still feel a sense of accomplishment.

Just get started

- **Not**: I can't write this speech until inspiration hits.
- **Instead**: I'll write what first comes to mind, then improve it later.

Look at what you have accomplished

- **Not**: I have hardly made a dent in all there is to do.
- **Instead**: I have reviewed my lecture notes and read three chapters. That won't guarantee me an 'A', but it's more than I did yesterday.

Be realistic!

- **Not**: I should be able to work full-time, be president of the golf club, spend more time with friends etc, etc with no trouble at all.
- **Instead**: I have limits. I can take on fewer responsibilities and still like myself.

Seven day procrastination plan

These are seven strategies you can use to eliminate procrastination. The suggestions are tied to the days of the week to help you recall.

On Monday, make it meaningful

Why is that job important? If you have been putting off something, take a minute to list all the benefits of completing the task. Look at the job in the perspective of your goals. Write down the task you have been avoiding, then, below it, write your reason for doing it. Relate the task to your goals, and be specific about the payoffs and rewards.

On Tuesday, take it apart

Break big jobs into small, manageable parts. Then be determined to complete one of those tasks. Make each task something you can accomplish in 15 minutes or less. Make the results measurable so you can see your progress. Give yourself a visual experience of getting something done.

On Wednesday, write an intention statement

Use an intention statement in conjunction with a small task you have created. Write your statement on a 3" x 5" card, and carry it with you or post it in your study area where you can see it often.

On Thursday, tell everyone

Announce your intention publicly. Tell a friend. Tell your spouse, roommate, parents, or children. Telling the world of your intention is an excellent technique to ensure its completion. Make the world your support group.

On Friday, find a reward

Rewards can be difficult to construct. A reward must be something that you would genuinely withhold from yourself if you did not earn it. Don't pick a movie as a reward if you plan to go anyway. If you don't complete what you set out to do, and go to the movie anyway, the movie would be an ineffective reward. When you legitimately reap your reward, notice how it feels. You may find that movies and reading are more enjoyable when you feel that you've earned it.

On Saturday, settle it, NOW

Do it now. The minute you notice yourself procrastinating, plunge into the task. Imagine yourself at a mountain lake, poised to dive. Gradual immersion would be slow torture. It's often less painful to leap.

Then be sure to savour the feeling of having the task behind you.

On Sunday, say no

Just say, 'No!' When you notice yourself continually pushing a task into the low-priority category, re-examine the purpose for doing it at all. If you realise that you really don't intend to do something, quit telling yourself that you will. That's procrastinating. Tell the truth and drop it. Then you're not procrastinating, and you don't have to carry around the baggage of an undone task.

You must liken this to your particular situation. You may need to make notes.

Procrastination: Ten ways to 'do it NOW'

Procrastination is a bad habit. There are two general causes – 'crooked thinking' (to justify our behaviour) and our behavioural patterns.

Crooked thinking reveals three major issues in delaying tactics – perfectionism, inadequacy, and discomfort. Those who believe they must turn in the most exemplary report may wait until all available resources have been reviewed or endlessly rewritten. Worry over producing the perfect project prevents them from finishing on time. Feelings of inadequacy can also cause delays. Those who feel that they are incompetent often believe they will fail and will avoid the unpleasantness of having their skills put to the test. Fear of discomfort is another way of putting a stop to what needs to be done. Yet, the more we delay, the worse the discomforting problem becomes.

Our behavioural patterns are the second cause. Getting started on an unpleasant or difficult task may seem impossible. Greater forces are required to start change than to sustain change. Another way of viewing it is that avoiding tasks reinforces procrastination which makes it harder to get things going. A person may be stuck too, not by the lack of desire, but by not knowing what to do. Overleaf are some ideas to break the habit. Remember, don't just read them, **do them**!

Remedies

1. Rational self-talk

Those old excuses really don't hold up to rational inspection. The 'two-column technique' will help. Write down all your excuses on one side of a piece of paper. Start challenging the faulty reasoning behind each of the excuses. Write down your realistic thoughts on the opposite side of each excuse. Here are two examples of excuses and realistic thoughts.

Excuse: I'm not in the mood right now.

Realistic thought: Mood doesn't do my work, actions do. If I wait for the right mood, I may never get it done.

Excuse: I'm just lazy.

Realistic thought: Labelling myself as lazy only brings me down. My work is really separate from who I am as a person. Getting started is the key to finishing.

2. Positive self-statements

Incorporate a list of self-motivating statements into your repertoire of thoughts. Consider...

'There's no time like the present.'

'The sooner I get done, the sooner I can play.'

3. Don't catastrophe

Jumping to the conclusion that you will fail or that you are no good at something will only create a wall of fear that will stop you cold. Recognise that your negative predictions are not facts. Focus on the present and what positive steps you can take toward reaching your goals.

4. Design clear goals

Think about what you want and what needs to be done. Be specific. If it's getting that work project completed by the deadline, figure out a time table with realistic goals at each step. Keep your sights within reason. Having goals too big can scare you away from starting.

5. Set up priorities

Write down all the things that need to be done in order of their importance. The greater the importance or urgency, the higher their priority. Put 'messing around' (distractions) in its proper place – last! Start at the top of the list and work your way down.

6. Split the tasks

Big projects feel overwhelming. Break them down into the smallest and most manageable subparts. This works especially well with the unpleasant jobs. Most of us can handle duties we dislike as long as they're for a short time and in small increments.

7. Get organised

Have all your materials ready before you begin a task. Use a daily schedule and have it with you all the time. List the tasks of the day or week realistically. Check off the tasks when you have completed them.

8. Take a stand

Commit yourself to doing the task. Write yourself a 'contract' and sign it. Better still, tell a friend, partner, or supervisor about your plans.

9. Use prompts

Write reminders to yourself and put them in conspicuous places like on the refrigerator, bathroom mirror and car dashboard. The more we remember, the greater the likelihood we'll follow through with our plans.

10. Reward yourself

Self-reinforcement has a powerful effect on developing a 'do it now' attitude. Enjoy the completion of even the smallest of tasks. Don't minimise your accomplishments. Go ahead, get started... **NOW**!

Go back through the list of things you procrastinate on, think about which of the ideas you can utilise.

When you go to work, pretend you do not know anything. What you will learn from asking and listening will save you a great deal of time.

Do it now!

Find things you can say to yourself which can actually kick you into action. Do it now, do it now, do it **NOW**.

Working smarter for managers

Work to precise and measured objectives: P.R.M objectives • Types of objective
Setting department result objectives: Defining result objectives for your department
Setting objectives for you
Review activity: Performance achievement • Assessing priorities • My job
Planning your time: Using your time effectively • A smart approach to planning
Working smarter as a manager: Recording time • Managing management time • Making the best use of time
Keeping a weekly time management log
Managing committed and usable time
Planning your time: Time allocation • Priorities • Length of consecutive time • Checking progress • Preparing a weekly plan
Types of management activity: Managing a department • Task review • Your authority
The first step: Diary keeping: Weekly time summary
Managing versus troubleshooting: Groups of activity • Check questions • Checklist – analysing your time
Delegation for managers: Giving authority • The desired results • Trust • Delegation • How to delegate successfully
Be a proactive time manager: Time – a resource • Where to start? • Symptoms of time management problems
Reactors versus planners: Support systems • Conclusion
Time management for managers – summary: Achieving our potential Creativity • Who owns the problem? • What can you do about it? • Key areas Defining the key areas • Using the key areas • Time stealers • Delegation Finding golden rules Appointments with me Conclusion

nine

Work to precise and measured objectives

P.R.M. objectives

At any level of activity whether it is in the overall running of the organisation, or in the day-to-day tasks that we perform ourselves, *it is essential to work to predetermined objectives*. Without objectives we are either fire-fighting or working to vague concepts such as experience, commonsense, etc. By establishing in advance precise objectives that have a result which can be measured, we know exactly where we are going and whether we are getting there. A good objective passes the three factor test – it is precise, it has a result and it can be measured (P.R.M.).

Types of objective

If working to objectives is to be meaningful, we must be specific; and we must identify different types of objective. There are three main types of objective for our purposes.

Output objectives

The result of this type of objective is either a physical object or a service provided by a department or individual. For example: 'Respond within 30 minutes to all 'urgent' maintenance request notes.'

Control objectives

Output objectives must be balanced by control objectives. For example: 'Urgent' maintenance requests should not comprise more than 20 per cent of the workload of the maintenance department.

Major change objectives

This objective relates to short or long-term changes. For example: 'To introduce the new incentive scheme by the beginning of the month.'

However, a very long list of objectives can cause confusion, for example:

- Having to work to too many objectives means that you can lose sight of priorities.
- The more objectives you add, the greater the likelihood of unnecessary overlap and duplication.

Setting department result objectives

One of the most effective, and perhaps the most essential actions for any manager is to set clear and effective objectives for departments and people in their domain.

> **Criteria for good objectives**
>
> 1. State required results, not actions, to achieve results.
> 2. Define measurable results.
> 3. Express objectives in clear, precise terms so that there is no risk of misunderstanding.
> 4. Be realistic.

Defining result objectives for your department

Follow the steps below to define result objectives for your department. That is, compile a comprehensive set of the results that your department should be achieving now.

Step 1

Jot down your department's key result areas, giving brief definitions of each of the different types of result you should achieve. These notes should cover or be grouped into three main areas:

1. **Outputs**: each of the different products or services you provide.
2. **Controls**: each of the measures that signify control of output achievement.
3. **Major change**: each present or impending major change.

A 'key result area' is best defined as a major or discrete performance focus for your business, division or department, eg productivity, sales, customer retention, loss prevention, etc.

Step 2

Define precise result objectives for each key result area in turn. Take care that each objective:

- produces a required result
- is capable of measurement
- is expressed in clear, precise terms
- is realistic.

Step 3

Check that your set of objectives presents a complete and clear picture of what you are required to achieve. You should note that key result areas refer to the specific products or services that you produce, eg a leisure and recreation department in a Local Authority could have separate key result areas for parks, baths, leisure centres, libraries, etc.

Tips on defining department/section result objectives

1. In each result objective define a required result, not an action to achieve results.
2. Each result objective must be capable of measurement or assessment. As you develop the definition ask yourself these questions:
   - Is it measured and reported now?
   - Can it be measured easily?
   - How do I know whether it is achieved?
3. If it is not possible to measure achievement or assess it objectively, try to express the result objective differently, in measurable terms.
4. Express each objective in precise, unambiguous terms so that anyone else reading or using the objective interprets it in exactly the same way as you.
5. The performance levels defined in objectives should be realistic, and challenging.
6. Don't define ideal performance levels that cannot be achieved.
7. Don't settle for slack performance levels that can be achieved with something to spare.
8. It is often possible to express result objectives in more than one way, for example either achievement of routine reports to schedule or achievement of report A by..., report B by..., etc. The second example is better. It provides a basis for monitoring performance more closely.
9. Review all objectives regularly, but don't change them unnecessarily.

Activity – Checking your objectives

Define your department's result objectives using the checklist opposite. List the objectives in the three areas of outputs, controls and major changes.

Do not spend a lot of time on this exercise. At this stage you should produce a rough draft only of the main result that your department seeks to achieve, and any performance shortfalls.

Department result objectives

Key point

1. Are all the main objectives listed, providing a complete picture of what the department is trying to achieve?

2. Do they cover the full range of outputs the department provides (both routine and non-routine outputs)?

3. Do they include objectives for controlling costs of achieving output? Do they include objectives for controlling quality?

4. Are objectives included for any present or impending major changes?

5. Does each objective define a result?

6. Does each objective define a performance level that can be measured or objectively assessed?

7. Can performance be measured or assessed easily? Is it measured now?

8. Is there an alternative objective which provides a better or more frequent measurement of your performance?

9. Are the performance levels stated in the objectives realistic?

10. Is each separate objective necessary (not covered by others in the list)?

11. Are all statements precise and unambiguous?

Notes

Setting objectives for you

The practice of working to results is equally important in the tasks you do yourself. These include:

- The regular supervisory tasks you carry out.
- Your liaison with other services and other departments.
- Any non-routine tasks you plan and carry out (eg performance and improvement plans). For each task you have to undertake ask yourself the basic question 'What results am I seeking?' and consciously work to these results as you do the task.

> **Example**
>
> ***Task***: You want to introduce a drive to improve work attendance in the department.
>
> ***Objective***: Rate of absenteeism in the department to be reduced from nine per cent to less than seven per cent of total available labour hours per week, by end of June.
>
> **Points to remember are:**
>
> 1. Define your aim – the result you want to achieve.
> 2. Include a performance level that can be measured or assessed.
> 3. Use precise, unambiguous language.
> 4. Each result must be an achievement or action (avoid non-actions like appreciation, knowledge, understanding, awareness).
> 5. Define specific rather than general performance levels.

Review activity

Look again at your list of result objectives. Review each result objective and test it against each item in the checklist on page 187. If necessary, rewrite your result objective.

Performance achievement

Record the actual performance achieved at the present time, comparing it with the result objective. You will probably find areas where current performance does not reach the result objective. In each case give the main reasons for this lower level of achievement.

Assessing priorities

In this exercise, rate various activities on three scales. Use values on each scale from zero to ten. The three scales are:

- Unimportant (0) to very important (10)
- Discretionary (0) to obligatory (10)
- Takes up little time (0) to very time-consuming (10).

My job

Classify each of the following activities, using the three scales.

Activity	1: Importance	2: Discretionary	3: Time usage
1. Making decisions: classifying, assessing facts, weighing alternatives, recommending or ordering a course of action.			
2. Achieving results through people; exercising interpersonal skills with subordinates and/or colleagues to further the objectives of the organisation. Now classify the following specific tasks in the same way:			
a. *Troubleshooting* ie finding causes for delays, mistakes, errors or below-standard work.			
b. *Forward planning* ie setting targets in some field of my activity for the next quarter.			
c. *Briefing subordinates* ie giving advice or instruction.			
d. *Conducting meetings* in the formal sense of calling staff and chairing the meeting.			
e. *Reviewing* the progress of subordinates.			
f. *Taking an interest* in personal problems perhaps making allowances for any domestic crisis. Wasted and lost time is a major cause of inefficiency amongst managers, and frustration amongst their staff.			

Planning your time

Using your time effectively

Planning is essential if you have to decide what to do for some, or all, of your time. Your plan can be on a monthly, weekly or daily basis. In developing your plan you have to take account of three types of activity:

1. **Routine or scheduled activity**.
2. **Immediate priority** – an unplanned action to deal with an urgent need.
3. **Open commitment** – an activity which is not scheduled or of immediate priority.

It is easy to plan routine or scheduled activities. However, immediate priorities present a problem since you cannot predict when each one will occur so you have to estimate the likely time taken with immediate priorities. You can then exclude this time when you produce a detailed plan for your open commitments.

A smart approach to planning

The following approach describes how you can plan your activities for a weekly period:

- Add up the total time used for routine and scheduled tasks.
- Record an estimate of the time needed for immediate priorities.
- Calculate the time that is left for open commitments.
- List your planned open commitments for the week, in priority sequence, estimating the time required and the day for each.
- Develop the list until you have used up all the time available for open commitments.

Operating and reviewing the plan

It is also important to record what you actually do in the week. In this way you can check the success of your plan. You can also use the information to improve your estimates of the time needed for immediate priorities and for scheduled and routine tasks. You can then make a plan for the next week.

Working smarter as a manager

Using your plan should give you a clearer idea of how you use your own time. Your effectiveness will be highlighted in the results you achieve. It may be enhanced by:

- concentrating on the things that really matter
- making sure that skills and specialisms are used to the full
- increasing delegation, thereby developing the skills of others and
- discovering how you work best as a person.

The following topics will cover aspects of the use of time: recording, management and consolidation.

> Do not over-control others. It is frustrating for them and time consuming for you.

Recording time

Time records can be kept in a self-recording diary or time log. These record every activity performed, usually by answering questions such as:

- What was the purpose of the activity?
- Where was the activity carried out?
- Were the other people superiors, subordinates, colleagues etc?

Managing management time

When we know how we spend our time we can think about how to manage it and where to direct our energy. As a manager you would do well to ask the following questions about every activity:

- Should it be done at all?
- When should it be done?
- Should it be delegated?
- To what extent should I be concerned with detail?

Manager's daily checklist

1. Am I giving enough attention to current activities, reviewing the past, and, especially, to planning the future?
2. Am I dividing my time correctly between different aspects of my job?
3. Have I allowed for the changes that have taken place in my job?
4. Who are the people I ought to be seeing?
5. How much time should I spend with each of them?
6. Do I plan my week, or do I only react to urgent problems?
7. Am I able to complete tasks or am I constantly interrupted?
8. Are the interruptions an essential part of my work?
9. What am I doing to further my own development?

Making the best use of time

The more senior you become, the more important it is to use time effectively. R. Stewart [2], a respected researcher into management effectiveness, identified five groups of managers based on their primary activities. They were:

- The Emissaries who spend much of their time in contact with the world outside.
- The Writers who spend more time on paperwork, tending to spend more time alone.
- The Discussers who spend more time with colleagues.
- The Troubleshooters whose work pattern is highly fragmented, coping with more crises than other managers.
- The Committee managers who spend more time with more than one person, and spend more time on personnel work.

Consider these findings and relate them to your own job. For example, are there conflicts between the demands of your job and the way in which you operate most effectively?

No matter how hard you try, the effectiveness with which you use your time is largely determined by others. While you are thinking about how you can make better use of your own time, also consider the effect you are having on the way that others use their time.

[2] R Stewart, *Managers and their Jobs*, Macmillan, 1967 and Pan Books, 1970

> **Consolidating time**
>
> One of the most serious problems is having insufficient time to plan. Stewart's research showed that the average manager had only nine half-hour periods alone during a four week period. To increase your available thinking time, it is important to consolidate the fragments of time that are truly your own into longer and more useful periods. How long they should be will depend on the balance between the manager's need for thinking time and the need to be accessible to colleagues. When planning time you should also ask yourself how you work best ie alone or with others or in the morning or afternoon.

Keeping a weekly time management log

Whilst a time log will benefit most people, it is invaluable for a manager whose time usage has a direct impact on the working routine and priorities of others. There are three stages to creating an effective time log record:

- List your key commitments and performance measures.
- Complete a weekly log.
- Prepare for a follow-up and review.

You must

- Now commit yourself to a date for review, listing your key commitments to improve your time management and delegation.

You should

- Make plans for your future week's work, and compare your actual performance with the plan.

- Use the plan and your actual performance to review your key commitments to improvement.

One week before the review

- You should assess your performance, using your plans and records.
- You should answer the questions in preparation for your follow-up.

Key commitments

Make a record of the following information that you will need for your follow-up exercise:

- Today's date
- The date of your time management and delegation review and follow-up.
- Your key commitments for improving your time management and delegation.

The weekly log

For each day of the week you should record, in 15 minute blocks:

- The way in which you plan to spend the day.
- Your actual tasks during the day.

You should record your activities showing the times when you are:

- Working alone.
- Planning alone.
- Dealing with correspondence.
- Dealing with interruptions.
- In discussions (saying who with).
- Dealing with personal matters.
- Supervising others.
- Telephoning.
- Travelling.
- Involved in other activities.

Preparing for the follow-up

In preparation for your follow-up you should ask yourself the following questions:

- What have you been doing to improve time management?
- What have been your most significant learning experiences?
- How do your colleagues view the effectiveness of your time management and delegation?
- How do your subordinates view the effectiveness of your delegation and time management?

Managing committed and usable time

The ability to manage time is partly determined by the amount of committed and usable time available.

Committed time

Committed time is time over which someone else has control, devoted to tasks committed for you. It can be system-committed or person-committed.

System-committed time is allocated by the system, eg wages are paid at 3 pm on Thursday. You have little influence on this time, though you might want to ask your superior to suggest changes which would be considered at a higher level.

Person-committed time is allocated by another person, usually your superior and is open to negotiation and you are free to approach your superior with alternative suggestions.

Usable time

You can decide what to do with usable time. This discretion may be absolute, so that you can use the time in any way you please, or conditional, for example when your superior tells you to finish a job by next week.

Time planning

As a step in managing time, you need to classify the time available into the following categories:

- System-committed time.
- Person-committed time.
- Usable time.

One way to do this is to keep a diary of one week's work, clarifying each task. For future weeks, complete a plan in advance. Show which category applies to each period of time on the plan.

Planning your time

Time allocation

When you have decided which parts of the week are *usable* time, you can allocate tasks to the *available* times. The two main factors to consider are the priorities to be given to each task. The length of consecutive time needed, or advisable, for each task.

Priorities

There are no fixed rules to determine priorities, but you should ask:

- What degree of urgency was implied by the instruction when the task was given? How long has the task been outstanding?
- How would delay in completing the task affect the work flow?
- What is the importance of the task in terms of human relations?

Length of consecutive time

Some jobs need to be completed in one sitting. Others can be completed in a number of short periods of time. In fact, it might be better to break some jobs up into small chunks, eg jobs that were physically tiring, extremely boring or very intricate.

Slack time

There will always be unexpected events which have to take immediate priority eg a machine breakdown or an unexpected delivery. Slack time must be available to allow for these events and the amount needed can only be judged by experience. Points to consider include:

- Never schedule every minute of every hour.
- Meal-times give a certain amount of slack in every day.
- Time outside normal working hours gives extra slack.
- Unused slack can give you time for unscheduled tasks.

It is useful to make a plan for the following week, which includes system-committed time, person-committed time and usable time.

Enter jobs into the usable time with a priority code for each one. Each day list up to five objectives which may relate to each classification of time.

Checking progress

Keep a record of the time needed to complete outstanding jobs. Record the average usable time available in each of the last four weeks. At least once a week compare the two figures. If the time needed is less than once the average usable time, you will probably be able to cope. If the time is more than twice the average usable time, you are soon likely to have problems.

Golden rules

1. Your aim must be successful completion of your objectives.
2. Non-productive time must be kept to a minimum.
3. Non-useful elements during productive time should be kept to a minimum.
4. Plan jobs so that they become simple routines or can be delegated.
5. Regularly compare the time needed to complete outstanding jobs with the average usable time available.

Preparing a weekly plan

Prepare a plan for using your time next week. Record the following:

- Scheduled and routine time committed.
- Time allowed for immediate priorities.
- Time available for open commitments.

List in order of priority the tasks that you hope to complete during the open commitment time.

- Give an estimate of the time that each task will take.
- Record the day on which you hope to complete each of the tasks.

As you work through the tasks during the week, record:

- The actual time you took to complete the task.
- The actual day on which you completed it.

At the end of the week, record the total time that you spent on open commitments. Now compare your plan with what actually happened during the week and write a review of your conclusions.

Types of management activity

Managing a department

The job of managers is to manage the resources under their control to achieve the required results.

The main categories of activities in managing a department are:

- planning the use of resources
- organising the use of resources
- leading and guiding subordinates
- controlling subordinates performance
- representing the department to customers, user departments, your boss, and others.

Each of the five main activities is described below.

1. Planning

This is the preparation for the short or long-term future. In planning, you establish future goals and determine a course of action to achieve them.

Planning includes:

- establishing future objectives
- scheduling
- budgeting
- plans for change in work organisation, location, layout, systems etc
- performance improvement plans, including action plans to raise departmental performance or individual coaching plans
- developing policies
- planning new procedures.

2. Organising

This involves making necessary arrangements to get things done.

Organising includes:

- making resources available
- allocating work
- arranging for tasks to be carried out
- establishing communication links.

3. Leading and guiding

These are concerned with man-management skills. They include:

- selecting people
- training, coaching and developing
- motivating
- handling industrial related issues
- counselling.

4. Controlling

Controlling means making sure that things get done properly eg:

- checking and reviewing department results
- monitoring or checking individual or group performance
- checking that delegated tasks have been completed
- checking how well systems are working
- ensuring that subordinates are conforming with legal and safety requirements.

5. Representing

This looks at how well you represent your department to:

- customers and user departments
- support services
- your boss
- senior management
- any other occasional contacts.

Task review

The headings described above cover most managerial activities. When you list the tasks that you carry out yourself, you may find that a number of tasks do not fit under any of the headings. Make a critical review of each of these tasks and ask:

- Should this be carried out by a manager?
- Who should do this task?

Assignment: The tasks you do

List the tasks you do in your job, under each of the headings below. Define the tasks that are specific to you.

Planning. Organising. Leading and guiding. Controlling. Representing. Any additional tasks.

Your authority

In any job it is important to be clear about the extent of your authority and the match between responsibility and authority.

For each of the tasks that you listed in the last exercise ('The tasks you do') identify the degree of authority you possess. Use one of four categories to show the degree of authority:

1. Delegate

You have full authority to carry out the task, but you normally delegate it to subordinates, guiding and controlling their actions.

2. Act

You have full authority to do this without consulting or reporting to your boss or anyone else.

3. Act under supervision

You have full authority to do this, but you are expected to report what you have done to your boss or another person.

4. Recommend

You have limited authority to make recommendations to your boss, or another person, but you cannot take major decisions yourself.

The first step: Diary keeping

Effective diary keeping is an essential first step in learning how to manage time. The method suggested is only one of many. Whatever method you use, it must record:

- what you planned to do during each day of the week, and
- what actually happened.

You will need to plan your time in 15 minute blocks. In each block, plan the times when you will be:

- working alone
- planning alone
- dealing with correspondence
- dealing with interruptions
- dealing with personal matters
- supervising others, telephoning, travelling and involved in other activities.

During your working day, record what tasks you actually did during each of the 15 minute blocks.

- How should I allocate my time between different activities?
- How can I make the best use of my time during an activity?

These can be discussed with colleagues.

Both the following questions can then be combined into a discussion on the topics:

What have I learned about making better use of my time?

How can I help myself and my staff to improve our use of time in the future?

Weekly time summary

Earlier you made a five day plan and record of your activities (see page 48-49). Use that record to answer the questions in this activity.

1. Did setting daily targets improve my effectiveness? In what ways did it help or hinder?
2. What was the longest period (other than travel) without interruption?
3. Which three interruptions were the most costly?
4. Could I have improved my use of time by any of the following means?
   - Eliminating unnecessary telephone calls. If so, how many?
   - Making telephone calls shorter or more effective.
   - Eliminating certain visits. If so, which?
   - Making visits shorter or more effective.
5. How much time was spent in:
   - Discussions?
   - Meetings?
   - How much of that time was necessary in each case?
   - What can I do to improve the effectiveness of my meetings and discussions?
6. How much time was spent on jobs which could have been delegated?
7. How much time was non-productive, for example, travel or personal time?
8. How much other time, apparently on tasks, was in fact non-productive?
9. Did my use of time improve during the time that I was using this record? If so, was the improvement qualitative, quantitative, or both?

Discuss your answers with colleagues and then answer the following question with a statement that you can present to the full meeting.

What two or three steps could I now take to improve my effectiveness in the use of time?

Managing versus troubleshooting

Groups of activity

In terms of the way you spend your time consider three groups of activity:

Routine or scheduled activities (R)

These are routine tasks, which you do at roughly the same time on a known day each week (eg production meeting) and scheduled tasks – commitments which you know about in advance, at least the week before.

Immediate priority activities (X)

These are activities for which there is no advance warning, but you have to handle them immediately when they crop up (eg major production line breakdown, sudden stoppage owing to industrial action, providing information requested urgently by plant manager).

Open commitment activities (O)

These are things which are not scheduled or of immediate priority, you fit them in when you can find the time (eg planning performance improvements, re-organising filing system, holding a coaching session with a foreman).

Check questions

Refer back to your weekly time record (page 49) to answer some of these questions:

1. How much of my time should be taken up by immediate priorities?
2. Are there any of these activities which I need not treat as immediate priorities?
3. Could some of these crises (immediate priorities) have been foreseen, prepared for or avoided?
4. How long are the chunks of uninterrupted time I can arrange to concentrate on important tasks?
5. Are they long enough?
6. Have I tackled my real priorities in my 'open commitment' time (my contributing objectives)?
7. Do I have enough 'open commitment' time to plan and make improvements?
8. Have I tended to put off unpleasant or boring tasks?
9. Which are the best days for putting in time on open commitments?

Notes

Checklist – analysing your time

Analyse how you spend your time and how you can improve. Answer them by referring to your record of how you spent the previous week at work.

Management activities

1. Am I giving the right balance of attention to each type of activity?
2. Can I cut down on jobs that do not need my skills?
3. Which of my tasks should be delegated?
4. Which activities could I train subordinates to do?

Controlling events

1. Am I spending too much time on immediate priorities?
2. Can some of these be treated in a less urgent manner?
3. Could some of these have been foreseen, and prepared for or avoided?
4. Am I able to stand back from the job and arrange long periods of uninterrupted time?
5. Are my open commitment tasks tackling my real priorities?

Contributing to results

1. Which of my activities show a poor return, through little or no contribution to results?
2. Should I revise my result objectives?
3. Which result objectives should I spend more time on?
4. Which result objectives should I spend less time on?

Notes

Delegation for managers

Giving authority

When delegating, the manager gives authority to the subordinate. The manager gives enough responsibility for the subordinate to perform the task. The subordinate accepts responsibility for the performance of the task but the manager keeps overall responsibility. For this reason, delegation can only be effective if it is linked with a system of control based on known targets and standards so that the manager can assess the results achieved.

Factors in delegation that also apply to the operation of any institution include:

- Policy – contributing effectively to the objectives of the enterprise.
- Organisation – providing everyone with work of adequate nature, scope and range.
- Procedures and techniques – ensuring that each person uses suitable tools or techniques.
- Technology – making sure that everyone works in an appropriate setting.
- Leadership effectiveness or motivation – giving everyone a chance to use their own specific skills.

The desired results

Used properly, delegation can result in:

- the advantages of specialisation
- freedom for the manager
- a defined pattern of responsibilities
- a system of training.

To be effective, delegation demands:

- explicit terms of reference
- full passing and acceptance of authority and responsibility
- an accepted and workable system of control
- freedom for the subordinate within their terms of reference
- an environment where everyone accepts the benefits of delegation.

Trust

The key to successful delegation lies in the trust between the manager and the subordinate. Trust relies on:

- mutual confidence in each other's ability, reliability and honesty
- working together to make trust grow
- the acceptance that trust is fragile
- a culture that encourages its growth.

Trust is increased if:

- the manager has some say in picking his subordinate
- the boundaries of the area of delegation are clearly defined
- control is directed towards ends not means
- parameters, objectives and control mechanisms are agreed jointly
- action is the responsibility of the subordinate.

Effective delegation depends on forethought and planning. Because two people are involved, it is necessary to plan in more detail and to use both manager and subordinate in the planning process.

Formalised delegation

The importance of delegation is recognised in most large organisations by the use of job descriptions. These lay down the tasks to be done, the duties and the responsibilities of the person employed. Unfortunately, this loses the idea that delegation is a contract between the manager and the subordinate. A job description can be criticised because:

- it applies to the job not the job holder, taking no account of their personal skills and aptitudes, and
- it becomes too rigid and does not apply to the everyday operational aspects of the job.

In contrast, delegation can combine flexibility with continuity and not become too rigid.

The need for delegation arises when a position becomes too busy or too complex. The manager tries to reduce the burden on time, energy or personal skills and passes over some of the workload. In all cases, the manager passes on certain duties while keeping overall responsibility. Note that we have used the words 'manager' and 'subordinate', but that it also possible for a task to be delegated upwards to a superior, or sideways to a colleague.

Delegation

Delegation can be considered a routine, almost inevitable factor associated with growth in size or complexity. In practice it is more complicated. Delegation can be to an individual, a team, a machine or to a system. However it is done, the overall responsibility rests with the manager. The manager is responsible for:

1. ensuring that the person is trained, competent and trustworthy
2. laying down precise terms and conditions of appointment
3. incorporating a system of accountability and control.

One problem can arise when the task is delegated to someone who is not a subordinate of the delegator. The following example shows how important it is to draft carefully the precise terms and accountability of the delegation, to clarify the relationship between the two people involved.

> **An example of upwards delegation**
>
> XYZ plc called in a consultant to look at profitability which was expected to be 15 per cent. The Sales Director had overall responsibility for pricing policy, and was being criticised because the overall level of profit was only 12 per cent. The consultant discovered that some large accounts had been delegated upwards to the Managing Director, who was only getting a profit of about two per cent. Even when the facts were pointed out to him, the Sales Director was hesitant about approaching the Managing Director and delegated the task to the consultant.

While travelling under light conditions, dictate letters or capture good ideas that come to you using a portable audio cassette recorder.

Delegating to technology

Even more difficult problems occur when work is delegated to non-humans. Increasingly, computers are taking over aspects of management previously carried out solely by staff responsible to the manager. Now the task is shared between the information provider, the software designer, the computer itself, and the person interpreting the results. In the short-term, this means that delegation must be very carefully designed to show the paths of accountability. In the long-term, it becomes a matter of organisational change and development.

How to delegate successfully

Most simply, use Peter Drucker's [3] method; get rid of anything that can be done by someone else. The main factors that stand in the way of such a simple solution are:

1. The delusion that only I can do that task.
2. A natural reluctance to relinquish any job that you enjoy doing.

[3] P F Drucker, *The Effective Executive*, Heinemann, 1967 and Pan Books, 1970

3. The difficulty in accepting that a job can be done satisfactorily by someone with less knowledge, skill or understanding.
4. Lack of understanding that delegation is a means of preparing subordinates for positions of greater responsibility.
5. Not understanding that a task is delegated to a person as well as to a position. When a new subordinate takes up a position, it is essential to review all delegation to match the tasks to the new person.
6. Failing to recognise the true nature of responsibility and accountability in a delegated task. The subordinate is accountable to the manager who retains overall responsibility to whatever superior authority exists.

Be a proactive time manager

Time – a resource

Time is the one resource that is available equally to all managers. However, it also causes considerable stress and concern to many. A survey by the Irish Management Institute, Dublin, showed that more than 80 per cent of managers considered that time was a problem for them.

Since your own use of time is tied to the effectiveness of those with whom you work, arrange a time management seminar for your entire organisation, so that you can mount a concerted attack on wasted time.

This resource will become even more difficult in the future, for two reasons:

- Managers will have more complicated choices to make between alternative uses of their time.
- The increasing size and sophistication of organisations raises critical issues for managing time, so that managers are increasingly open to demands from others on their time.

While some organisations are being redesigned to cope, the burden of choosing boundaries and use of time still rests with the individual manager.

Where to start?

The first step is to get a clear understanding of the problem, and only then to look at possible solutions. Managers also need to realise that they may have an investment in their own problem, and may be reluctant to change. Understanding the problem is partly a question of knowing where to start. The Dublin survey showed that most managers could identify the 'secrets of good time management':

- Establish goals and priorities
- Make time to do planning
- Delegate all unnecessary work
- Allocate and schedule time to important and priority activities.

These secrets are very similar to the solutions to be found in the literature. However, the same managers still have problems with time management in their work. It would appear that the problem is more complex.

Symptoms of time management problems

The five most common symptoms were:

- Frequent interruptions from other people or the telephone.
- Not getting enough time to plan.
- Not getting as much done as I could or should.
- Having to clear up my subordinates' problems too often.
- Having to work long hours.

Even at this stage, it is clear that the problem is complex. For example, managers feel that they do not get enough time to plan, but also feel that they spend too much time dealing with unnecessary interruptions.

Reactors versus planners

To look at the real issues causing the symptoms, it is necessary to look at the reasons why many managers behave as 'reactors' rather than as 'proactive planners'.

Ambiguity

For many managers, a large part of the problem is caused by the ambiguity of their job. H Beric Wright[(4)] lists role ambiguity as one of the six most common executive stress factors. For many managers the issue of '**what does the organisation want from me?**' is replaced by the question '**what should I do to keep in a job?**'

Managers in the survey were asked to describe their jobs. 95 per cent responded by giving their job title or a list of responsibilities, rather than their function.

Getting results

A second part of the problem is involved with the idea of 'getting results'. Though 80 per cent of managers suggested goal and priority setting as essential to good time management, fewer than 45 per cent actually had clear objectives and priorities in their jobs.

The nature of time

The third part of the complex problem involves the nature of time itself. Time rushes by when we are enjoying ourselves, but passes very slowly when we are bored or tense. Consequently, there is often a large discrepancy between the time that managers estimate they spend on each task and the actual time taken.

Fragmentation

The fourth part of the problem is the fragmented nature of a manager's work. Research has found that half the things a

[(4)] B H Wright, *Executive Ease and Dis-Ease*, Gower Press, 1975

manager does are of less than nine minutes duration. However, many of the important things that a manager does require large chunks of time. The survey showed that managers want to spend more time on:

- planning future policies and activities
- staff development and training
- keeping up-to-date with new developments
- developing new ways of working.

All four of these activities require the lengthy periods of time that are not normally available to a manager.

Time-wasters

These include telephone interruptions, meetings and unnecessary paperwork. However, time-wasters can be a cover under which harassed executives hide, meetings can be arranged too often, for example. It is also a fact that many executives want to be interrupted, and may create interruptions themselves.

The problem

These interrelated problems all give the manager a feeling of being controlled rather than controlling, which makes the situation stressful. The skill of time management begins with the realisation that the obstacles and pressures of time are there to be managed. The place to start is with the problem.

Data

One way to start is by getting data about current use of time. The most commonly accepted method is to keep a diary or time log. An analysis of how time is spent over a couple of days is usually startling, and often uncomfortable. It can, by itself, often show the way forward.

Other approaches include an analysis of the manager's job description, or a list of activities. This can show the time taken on priority activities, possible activities which can be delegated and managerial, as opposed to operating, activities. Specific problems such as interruptions can be analysed in the same way.

Stress points

An alternative starting place is to look at the stress points in the job. Much job-related stress is connected with feelings that the job is unclear, frustrating or under-productive. Many managers feel that they are unable to influence the situation and blame factors outside their control. For many managers, an appropriate place to start is by asking one of the following questions:

1. What frustrates me about my job?
2. What do I want from my job?
3. What am I doing too much, or too little, of?
4. What do I want to say 'no' to?
5. What are my priorities?

An important part of solving the problem is to identify what can be controlled, rather than putting frustrated energy into the uncontrollable. In dealing with stress, it is important to recognise the areas in the job where choices can be made.

Support systems

Confronting the problem of poor time management is difficult for managers to do alone. It may need the help of others close to the manager. Support systems (such as Weight-Watchers or Alcoholics Anonymous) provide a potential for feedback, guidance and understanding. Managers might give some thought to the quality of their support systems:

- Do my boss and I agree about the best use of my time?
- Do I spend enough of the right kind of time with my boss, subordinates, secretary?
- Who is in my support system?
- Do I get the right amount of time with them?

Managers who feel that they have an inadequate support system may choose to do things themselves. However, effective time-managers seem to learn that it is better to develop effective support systems. This often means that less time is spent producing immediate tangible results, but more time is spent creating better systems for producing results in the longer term. These longer term aims are likely to mean that the manager spends more time with certain individuals or groups.

Conclusion

Few managers are intuitively good at managing their time, most have to work at it. It is a learned skill. There are two popular myths regarding time management:

- A manager's time is controlled by external events.
- There are procedures available which easily ensure good time management.

The true skill of time management lies somewhere between these two myths. Managers need to start by getting a better understanding of the problem. Here are some suggestions as to possible methods:

- Collecting data.
- Looking at stress factors.
- Assessing the available support systems.

Moving towards better time management involves an incremental development of knowledge and skill, rather than any instant cure. The real solutions lie in identifying the true nature of the problem and learning ways of dealing with it that are acceptable remedies for the manager.

Time management for managers – summary

It is important to stand back from the problem and look at:

- your job description
- your desk
- time stealers
- delegation.

Achieving our potential

Modern managers are questioning and critical of information and ideas presented to them. This is also true of the experienced managers who have influenced our understanding of human relationships and behaviour in a changing industrial and commercial world. These effective managers have a major influence on the total effectiveness of the organisation. In a world that shows a greater accent on the individual, the manager needs to look further ahead than the immediate problems and to start planning to be a total human being. This plan must include work, family, friends, and personal interests.

Sportsmen practise regularly to stay proficient in their field. So should managers. This can begin with the question, '**What do I need to do to be more effective?**' The manager will then have taken the first step that leads to more achievement and less stress.

Creativity

One of the key factors in realising our potential is to have a basic understanding of our greatest resource – our brain. The left hand side of our brain gives us our logic. It is where we evaluate against experience. The right hand side gives us our creativity. Western education has relied heavily on dominance of the left hand side. Increasingly, however, managers have to be creative in their thoughts and actions. To be effective the manager must look at problems logically and be creative.

Who owns the problem?

We all know what we should be doing, but too often we let outside influences control our work. This can cause frustration, but it is important to note that it may not be the only cause. Other causes may include:

- a problem at home
- finding time to meet an important deadline
- lack of co-operation from colleagues, or lack of clarity about responsibilities.

You may also have fallen into bad work habits. These may be because:

- your workload has increased
- you do not delegate sufficiently.

These factors may reduce your effectiveness and increase your sense of frustration.

What can you do about it?

How often do you, as a busy manager, sit back and take stock?

Do you ask the questions:

- How do I spend my working day?
- What are my personal and career objectives?
- How do the objectives in the two areas link together?
- How do the answers to these three questions influence my use of time?

Key areas

To change your way of working, you must keep a clear view of your personal and career objectives. You will then be better able to cope with situations which are difficult, stressful or time-delaying and have a clear perspective when answering the question 'What do we do now?' You can begin to define your objectives by establishing the key areas of your private and working life. Choose about nine areas on which you need to concentrate your time and energy to achieve your goals. Look for areas in which you hope to achieve results. Since your main emphasis will be on work, you will probably allocate six or seven areas to work and the remainder to your private life. Key areas should not describe the results you want to achieve, but the areas within which you want results.

Defining the key areas

A quick look at your job description might help you to define the key areas. Other methods could include listing and classifying all your daily work activities, or asking yourself what would happen if your position or department was abolished. In each case you can identify the overall requirements of your job and then ask yourself which key areas you need to concentrate on to achieve your goals.

Using the key areas

Having written down the key areas, you should consult them from time to time. Consider whether the decisions you take contribute to your objectives. You may find that defining your key areas helps when you have to decide what priority to give a particular task.

Your desk

Take a look at the organisation of your desk and paperwork:

1. Piles of paper on the desk generate a feeling of not being up to date. They will force you to think of more than one job at a time.
2. In and out-baskets for paper work are essential for effective working.
3. Operate a strict policy of constantly emptying your in-tray and deciding immediately what actions to take.
4. A desk file is also useful, with drawers to divide work into papers requiring immediate action, action within a week, awaiting information etc.
5. Throw away anything you will do nothing about.
6. Set deadlines for every job. Stick to them.
7. Go through your drawers at regular intervals.
8. When you are interrupted, put the papers you are working on in the correct drawer before starting a fresh task.
9. Do easy tasks when you only have a short time available, or when you are likely to be interrupted.
10. File each piece immediately in the right place.
11. Only have one task on your desk at any time.

Time stealers

Time stealers are the most important obstacles that bar your way to achieving your objectives. In some cases the problem may be outside your control, but if you know the cause it may reduce the negative effect on you. To identify time stealers, list the main obstacles which adversely effect your performance, together with possible solutions. Examples associated with the telephone might include:

- **discussion too lengthy**: separate chat from information
- **unwanted calls get through**: discuss this with your secretary/colleagues and make a plan.

You may find that the vast majority of time stealers are of your own making. If this applies to you, you may have to change your attitude. It is most unlikely that you will change others; you can only change yourself.

Delegation

Delegation is a contentious point. Few managers like to think that they are bad at this, for poor delegation often means poor managerial ability. Any system of delegation must follow logical concepts and techniques – there are no simple solutions, only general guidelines. All delegation needs to be carefully planned, but the manager must remember that the test of any management system is whether it works in practice.

Always delegate slightly more than what you feel the subordinate is capable of handling. You will love the pleasant surprises, and the failures will be few in number.

Finding golden rules

There are no easy answers to the management of time, but two things are clear:

- The manager's own commitment is vital.
- The manager's attitude must be positive.

If both these conditions exist, a proper system can be implemented to ensure continuity of effort. An effective system should include certain golden rules.

Some golden rules for managers

1. Never postpone important matters that are unpleasant.
2. Establish a fixed daily routine.
3. Do jobs requiring mental effort when you are at your best.
4. Fix realistic deadlines for all jobs and stick to them.
5. Put off everything that is not important.
6. Occasionally, analyse your interruptions.
7. Do one thing at a time.
8. Plan your telephone calls whenever possible.
9. Set definite times or meetings to discuss routine matters.
10. Be selective.
11. Learn to say 'No'.
12. Make a regular check on your use of time.
13. Establish realistic working goals.
14. Avoid taking work home unless you are sure you will do it.
15. Treat a large job as a series of small, achievable tasks.

Appointments with me

Managers wishing to get better control of their time during the day can book appointments with themselves. This may be short, to take stock of progress, or longer for specific key tasks.

Conclusion

Beware that the very simplicity of some of these ideas does not hide their effectiveness. Achievement in management is highly stimulating.

Miscellaneous tips and ideas

Working in a 'virtual office': Overwork • Procrastination

Working at home: Developing routines when working at home • Developing systems of work at home

Ideas for successful motoring

Ideas for successful travelling – hotels

Ideas for successful travelling – airlines

Career development: Activities

Action learning and learning to learn: Self assessment – you and your job • Personal profile

Using a log book for action learning: Completing the log book

Career planning in a time of change: You are not your job or work • Virtual employment • Career planning action plan

Working in a 'virtual office': Overwork • Procrastination
Working at home: Developing routines when working at home • Developing systems of work at home
Ideas for successful motoring
Ideas for successful travelling – hotels
Ideas for successful travelling – airlines
Career development: Activities
Action learning and learning to learn: Self assessment – you and your job • Personal profile
Using a log book for action learning: Completing the log book
Career planning in a time of change: You are not your job or work • Virtual employment • Career planning action plan
Working in a 'virtual office': Overwork • Procrastination
Working at home: Developing routines when working at home • Developing systems of work at home
Ideas for successful motoring
Ideas for successful travelling – hotels
Ideas for successful travelling –

ten

Working in a 'virtual office'

This section will help you identify and design self-management systems that succeed for you when you are working from home.

First, expect a 30 to 90 day acclimatisation period when you start teleworking. It takes a while to figure out how to manage time, space, communication systems and projects while working in two locations or from home.

Overwork

Once you start teleworking, you will have 24-hour access to work. At the office, routines structure your time. When teleworking though you may not know when to stop. Simply putting in more hours does not make you more effective. Establishing business hours for your work-at-home days, informing your colleagues of these hours, and sticking to them are major steps toward balancing work with other parts of your life. If you have a tendency to overwork, it will take practice and discipline to limit your working hours.

Procrastination

The opposite of work addiction is procrastination and lack of motivation. When you work at home, there's no one to supervise you or recognise that you've put in a good day's work.

Are you sometimes motivated to work and at other times procrastinate?

Pay attention to when you procrastinate, what things act as distractions, what tasks you tend to put off. Once you have an idea why you procrastinate, you can learn to outsmart yourself (this could include fear of success or failure; rebellion; anxiety or loneliness).

Working at home

Developing routines when working at home

One of the best ways to overcome a lack of motivation is to get into specific routines.

Motivation

Setting a schedule is very helpful. Clear hours of business are good for overcoming both work addiction and lack of motivation.

If you have a task to do and simply cannot get motivated, try doing another work-related task which may prepare you for the original one. If that doesn't work, try doing something else entirely.

Learn how to motivate yourself. Do you like to work in a clean, neat workspace? Tidying it up might help get you started. Calling the office when you first sit down at your desk might help – it will remind them that you are working at home, not taking a day off.

Task-oriented systems

Perhaps you envisioned teleworking as a way to do your creative work at home and the mechanised tasks at the office where the interruptions won't bother you as much, but there are still times when you have to work on boring tasks at home. Some people feel they ought to do the least-liked tasks first. If you are motivated to do a certain task now, don't wait until later to do it. When you've done as much as you can, or run out of energy, or come to a natural stopping point, then is a good time to do the parts you are less enthusiastic about. You can use the momentum of the fun project to carry you through the boring task.

Reward systems

If reward systems work for you, decide what rewards are most effective such as coffee or tv breaks. Remember, the point of these rewards is to ***motivate*** you to work. Don't give yourself the reward before you've achieved your goal.

Positive reinforcement

Positive reinforcement is a good motivating tool. Think of the things you say to yourself when you use negative 'self-talk'. Now reverse them. Say them with conviction. Check your energy level and see how you feel. If you have put as much energy into this exercise as you have into negative self-talk, you should feel more energised and motivated.

Developing systems of work at home

> Discuss time management with your boss and work colleagues and determine what you can do as individuals and as a team to use time more effectively. Don't imagine that it is just you that finds it a challenge.

Working at home means being able to create and follow effective structures which take the place of those at the office. Some people are most comfortable with systems and routines very much like those they use at the office.

Some telecommuters prefer to schedule their day with firm starting and stopping times. Others build in flexibility. They count backwards from project deadlines and make careful daily and weekly schedules for what they need to accomplish. They work until they've met their goals for each day, then quit. Others don't like schedules at all and on their teleworking days they may not get started until afternoon, and keep working until late at night. Some people thrive on this. For others, it can be a source of stress as they waste productive hours, then rush frantically to stay on target.

To be successful as a telecommuter, you need to be aware of your goals and target everything you do toward meeting them.

Be flexible enough to recognise that when something isn't working for you, it's up to you to change it until it does work. For example, if you feel you need more input from your manager, ask for it.

When you structure everyday activities into routines, you save time and energy for decision-making at a creative level. Why waste time searching for information when you can devise a filing system that is easy to use? There may be times when your routine gets disrupted by an unanticipated event. That's fine, just get back to it as soon as you can.

Get a lock put on the door of the room that is your home office. You can use it to lock yourself in... and out!

Periodically, check your routine to see if it's working. Systems should make your life easier, not more complex. If you are not getting the results you want from your routine, revise it.

The flexibility of working at home a few days a week can be stimulating. Harness that flexibility and make it work for you.

How many hours will you work at home each day and week?

You can limit your tendency to overwork or motivate yourself to work harder by deciding this up front.

Which hours will you work?

When working at home, 9-5 may not suit your needs. Set a schedule for your work-at-home days and inform those people who will be affected by that decision.

How many breaks will you take during the day?

Figure out if you work best with frequent short breaks or longer breaks at longer intervals, but do take breaks. Telecommuters need to be disciplined and self-motivated. Severe headaches, eyestrain, neck and back pain are the result of working too long without a break. If you have this problem, try setting an alarm clock to go off every two hours or so. When it goes off, force yourself to get up and stretch, look away from the screen, or do some neck and back exercises. You can still think about work while you're stretching, but give your body a break.

When will you do household chores?

Some people feel they cannot work in a house that is less than spotless, so they spend time cleaning instead of working. This is a good reason to have a separate room for your home office. Try keeping just that room clean. **Beware**: the people you live with may expect you to do more housework 'now that you're home anyway'. Remind them that you are at home to work. You may find that doing one household chore per work-at-home day is a good compromise.

When will you eat when you work at home?

Make a conscious decision about this. Schedule regular lunch breaks to avoid excessive snacking or not eating at all.

When and how will you dress when you work at home?

Some people like to wear jeans and a T-shirt, but others find that if they dress too casually, their attitude seems to relax and they can't get down to work. Dressing for work at home the same as you do for the office may be the best solution.

If you have children, when will you be available to them?

Teleworking is not a substitute for childcare. Children need a lot of attention and have a right to expect it from you. But your work needs attention too. Make arrangements for childcare, and set boundaries on your availability to kids and others.

What interruptions will you allow?

There will be phone calls from friends as well as co-workers, plus deliveries, repair service calls, neighbours, etc. It's better to define a policy in advance so you don't have to make individual decisions at each distraction.

Ideas for successful motoring

1. Plan your journey well – consider the quantity and quality of customer's vs journey time and distance. How or when else could I service this account? Who else could I see?
2. Travel off-peak – travel before or after the rush-hours or plan your journey to travel in the opposite direction to the main flow.
3. Fill up with petrol when you don't need it – Murphy's Law says that you will run out on the way to an important call, when you are already late, and can't find a garage.
4. Listen to educational tapes or classical music whilst driving – use the time to learn new skills with audio-tapes. Alternatively, listen to classical music, it will help you get through the day and the traffic with less fatigue and greater composure.
5. The faster you drive – the faster you get tired – driving at 90 mph requires about twice the concentration, and creates more noise and vibration than 70mph.
6. Never drive more than about an hour and a half without a break – stretch, walk around, get some fresh air, even for just a few minutes.
7. Carry a good map, and invest in the A-Zs of the towns and cities you visit most frequently. Write out your route on paper in advance. Allow buffer time – and carry work with you to do when (if!) you arrive early.
8. Never travel more than 30 minutes from the office without confirming an appointment by phone the day before – even if you have confirmed it in writing.
9. Don't play 'head' games at 70 mph. Next time you catch yourself cutting someone up or yelling abuse at them, imagine it is one or your best customers – and they recognise you!!
10. Never drink and drive. There is no safe level of alcohol.

Ideas for successful travelling – hotels

1. Book in advance, by fax if you can. Join one of the corporate card schemes – they can make things just a little bit easier.
2. Be choosy about your room. Ask for what you want – non-smoking or a quiet room. Watch out for rooms next to car parks, kitchens, night-clubs or boiler rooms.
3. Don't vegetate – exercise or educate. Don't just waste an evening because you're on your own – take the time to read or exercise.
4. Find your favourite hotels. A familiar face, environment and known level of service can take the drudgery out of travelling and staying away.
5. If the hotel you want to stay in is full, ask to be put at the top of the list for cancelled rooms and tell them that you'll call back (at an arranged time) to check.
6. When making single restaurant reservations – ask if there are any other single diners, and then see if the head waiter could ask them if they would mind sharing a table. If nothing else, you might liven up an otherwise dull evening – and perhaps make some new contacts.
7. Avoid the check-out bottle-neck – ask them to forward the account – or get them to take a card imprint and sign it before breakfast.
8. Hotel lounges make great daytime meeting places – develop good relationships at the hotels you intend to use regularly. Always order coffee and tea – but don't abuse the service.
9. Expect good service – and always compliment it.
10. Make sure they spell your name correctly – and ask how they communicate messages.

Ideas for successful travelling – airlines

1. Travel light, make sure your luggage is distinctive so you can recognise it easily on the reclaim belt, but not obviously flamboyant to attract pilfering or customs.
2. Sleep, relax or work on planes, in that order.
3. Adjust to other time zones immediately, just act as if these were your normal hours; eat meals and sleep in the new time only. Alter the time on your watch as soon as you take off.
4. When you book your flight, reserve your seats as near to the front of the aircraft as possible.
5. Avoid alcohol; it speeds up dehydration and can lower your energy levels. Drink plenty of water during and after any flight.
6. Refuse, in advance, to be annoyed by delays or inconveniences. Have plenty of things to do/read/think about in case of delay.
7. Wherever possible travel off-peak, evening flights usually mean a full day's work before you leave, and the airports and roads are often quieter at night or in the early hours of the morning.
8. Strike up conversations with fellow passengers; as well as excellent practise of your conversational skills, it can make journeys pass quicker, and often leads you to some interesting people.
9. Travel in loose comfortable clothes and change when you arrive at your destination. The longer the flight, the more important this is.
10. Eat light for 24 hours before flying and when travelling. Most airlines offer vegetarian dishes, which you can request when booking your ticket. These meals are usually easier to digest. On longer flights take some fruit – apples are ideal – these are excellent for energy and replacing lost fluid.

Career development

Included in this section are several questionnaires that will help you make an assessment of your current competencies. This may be a new concept to you but it is important that you understand its meaning and its implications. By the end of the section you should have begun to be aware of your development needs and started to prepare items for your development plan.

Activities

1. Prepare your CV

Draw up a curriculum vitae listing your key result areas, achievements and training. Pay particular attention to the key result areas of each job title and your achievements in that job. Include a one-paragraph description of yourself as you are now. Is there a developing pattern about how your skills have emerged, eg 'I've learned a lot by changing jobs every two years.'

2. Identify your starting point

Look at your job systematically in terms of current skill and knowledge requirements. Look at a current job description, job specification and key result areas.

3. Draw up a seven-point plan of the ideal person to fill your job

- How does this person differ from you?
- If you could wave a magic wand, what would you change about yourself?

You now need to look at your job systematically in terms of both future skill and knowledge requirements:

Do you have access to the organisation's Business Plan or the Human Resource Plan?

This should give you clues to the type of managers required in the future. If this is not available, try to talk to senior people about how they see the future of the organisation. We are not talking about changes in specific departments here, but in those skills that will affect all members of staff, for example if all managers had to run profit centres their attitude to budgeting, etc would be quite different. If all managers were given personal computers, they would need greater information technology skills. We are trying to assess these future changes in your job.

Always keep your CV up to date, you never know when you might need it.

Look at the external factors that might affect your job in the future

Factors can include legislation, technology and the economy. Write down some of the things that occur to you. Talk to people who might know more.

Action learning and learning to learn

You may never be aware that you are learning. On the other hand you may sometimes be very aware of it. Somehow it has percolated into the subconscious. In fact, we are all learning all of the time, but in a rather disjointed, hit-and-miss way.

Self assessment – you and your job

- What parts of your job do you really like?
- Do you think that you are in the right job?
- How can you manage yourself better?

These are some of the questions we shall look at to encourage you to think actively about your approach to work.

Keep a notebook, labelled 'Learning Log'. At the end of each day jot down what you have learned. It is impossible to finish a day having learned less.

Understanding why it is that you consciously avoid certain parts of your job, or find more opportunities to undertake the other aspects of the work that you prefer, can help you to 'manage' yourself more effectively. Very often we find some aspects of our job really exhilarating and we become very enthusiastic about that type of work. At other times we become lethargic and find particular aspects of the job really 'boring'. Based on the concepts of Team Management Systems developed by Charles Margerison and Dick McCann, this section will help you draw up plans to operate better in yourself and with others in a more effective and efficient manner.

Personal profile

Each of us has a self image that influences the way we work and relate to people. Each day at work we make assessments of each other and use this in our interpersonal dealings. Describe how you see yourself in the work situation.

1. What are the key words or phrases that you feel best describe you at work? What are your strengths and weaknesses? Try to look at yourself objectively and record key characteristics.
2. List the main requirements of your job.
3. In what areas of your work do you feel you have particular strengths?
4. What are the areas of your job in which you feel less strong?
5. What aspects of your work do you like best? (Think of your current job as well as past jobs.)
6. What aspects of your job do you like least? (Think of your current job as well as past jobs.)

Notes

Personal profile *continued*

7. In what parts of your job would you say you perform best?
8. What parts of your job need working on if you are to improve your performance?
9. What do you think you have learned most from your previous jobs?
10. How would you describe the people with whom you work best?
11. How would you describe the people with whom you find it difficult to work?
12. How would you like to develop and improve in your work in the future?

Notes

Using a log book for action learning

Objectives

Most people have plenty of experiences, but they often do not learn as fully from them as they could. It is a valuable idea to keep and use a 'Log Book' so that you can identify useful learning experiences, develop your learning and undertake actions as a result.

Completing the log book

Keep an 'evidence' file – copies of letters, reports, statistics, work of any kind that demonstrate your achievements and competence.

1. The form in which you keep the Log Book should reflect the objectives above, ie the Log Book is not solely a record but is a means of securing action.
2. You will find that there are different occasions when entries should be made, eg during and immediately after an experience, meeting or discussion.
3. Record *significant* events only. You may be able to identify an important experience in advance, or you may recognise after the event that something significant (to you) has occurred.
4. Such events may occur within the formal context of the resource or outside it. The process of collecting information from colleagues for a section or for written assignments may be equalled by similar experiences at your place of work. In the same way, your record of interesting learning from resource related discussions should be paralleled by your experience from other projects or group discussions. This integration of learning, both from this resource and from normal work experience, is a significant objective of the Learning Log.
5. Take time to capture small details that may be significant when combined together. You may have learned something in terms of content, 'the meeting demonstrated the kind of benefits sought by that customer,' or process, 'I saw how the Chairman handled some difficult interventions. He made everyone happy by... '
6. Weekly review to assess the previously unconnected experiences recorded earlier. The review will probably consist of a summary of main points, or conclusions from a number of events.

   You will certainly benefit from reviewing your Log with your colleagues after major tasks, assignments and projects.

   Try to make your review explicit against your action plan, rather than general. For example, instead of simply noting that you did not learn from a particular experience, try and analyse why (perhaps by looking at your own behaviour, not that of others).

Those of you with a high Activist and low Reflector score will probably find the disciplined approach outlined here uncomfortable, and perhaps initially unrewarding. Have patience and persevere – a number of high Activists have said that in the end the process was very important for them.

Career planning in a time of change

It is estimated that soon over a third of the population will not have regular, full-time employed positions as we have experienced in the past. This means that we need to become familiar with uncertainty and change, recognising that a typical career for your future may be distinctly different from the one considered in the past.

For example, a major bank used to have 38 grades, one promotion every two years from college to retirement. Today, they would only expect a handful or employees to still be with the organisation after ten years, and even then possibly doing a completely different job.

A Career's Advisor recently spoke at a meeting of parents, and told them not to worry about what their children would be doing in ten or 20 years time. He explained, 'The job probably hasn't been created yet and would be using technology that has not yet been introduced.'

You and your career in the new millennium

What is a 'career'? *The Shorter Oxford Dictionary* says that it is 'a person's progress through life, a profession offering opportunities for advancement'. It is unlikely that anyone would argue with the first part but there may have to be some rethinking about the word 'advancement'. This has come to mean ever upwards and onwards with a salary level and other rewards to match. This may not be so in the future.

Most of us in the western and industrialised nations have grown-up with the following understandings, gained from our culture and experience:

- Do your work well and keep your job.
- Work hard and you will be rewarded.
- Loyalty of service is rewarded and recognised by promotion and salary increases.

- The more staff, accounts or people you have to look after, the greater your prestige and remuneration.
- Companies and organisations that employ people look after them, generally speaking.
- Get a trade and you'll be okay.
- The larger the employer the safer your position, the government being the most secure of all.
- Keep your head down and don't rock the boat.

However, the reality of today's and tomorrow's workplace, and hence career, is very different, the new code might include:

- Become a mercenary – work for the person or organisation who will pay you the most.
- Expect no loyalty from your organisation. Organisations have now renamed their personnel department to HR – Human Resources. You are just a 'resource', no different from a desk, a computer or company car.
- Work for yourself – even if you're on a company payroll. At the end of the day, we are all working for ourselves.
- Be ready to change jobs regularly – out of need or desire. Keep your CV constantly updated and network frequently.
- Build value by constantly increasing and upgrading your own skills and knowledge, not by seeking to manage larger groups of people.
- You will be paid more when you are worth more, not because you've been there longer. In the 'new' world, length of service might become a liability not an asset. Younger, fresher, and probably cheaper, staff may be more attractive to employers, unless you can offer more than just experience.
- Consider a complete career change once or twice. Who ever said that just because we picked one area of interest in our late teens or early twenties we couldn't change our minds.
- Get on your bike! This phrase, made famous during the eighties by a Conservative politician has some relevance if you ignore the political slant. If the industry trades, profession, town, district or even country you are in lacks the opportunity or future – move, change and adapt. If the car

factory closes down, buy a PC and learn to type or buy an apron and learn to cook!

- The larger the employer the more unsafe your position is. Smaller companies run mean and lean, always have and always will probably. Large organisations have had to learn this. However, they are like dinosaurs, by the time a thought leaves the brain and transmits down to a muscle to act, the moment is lost. The next decade could see some dramatic changes to the way we live and work; to be forewarned is to be forearmed.
- Rock the boat occasionally, at least you'll get noticed.
- Don't rule out really working for yourself. Resign and ask you company to hire you as a freelance consultant.

There is a glut of managers and many organisations are cutting their hierarchies to remain competitive. Today's managers may have to settle for a career where their skills and knowledge widen and deepen; where they may have more and different responsibilities but not in the hierarchical sense. This section is intended to get you thinking about your organisation (and whether you fit it) and what it might be like in the future. It is also intended to make you look at the future in terms of what might bring satisfaction other than an executive parking-space.

You are not your job or work

One of the most difficult changes that we can make is to our own self-image or self-identity. These changes are often put upon us by events as we progress through life – we get married, get divorced, don't get married, acquire more money and status symbols, have children, move to a different area, lose our job, gain different jobs. One of the strongest cultural ties is the association we have with our profession, job or trade. For example, when asked 'What do you do?' or 'Who are you?' by a stranger, we will often label ourselves as a 'programmer' or an 'accountant' or 'I work in publishing'. The truth is you are a great many things as an individual, you work to earn a living.

In the future you may have several different types of job over a number of years, or at the same time. You might find yourself working constantly on a series of short fixed-term contracts, maybe with breaks in-between. However, you might also find that the job that you do to earn a living is difficult to define – already terms such as 'knowledge worker' and 'research engineer' or 'software wizard' are being used.

Increasingly your main job, how you choose to earn a living, might not be how you choose to define yourself. For example, you might work in a telephone call centre during the day, but your real passion is athletics or painting, which you might do on a semi-professional basis.

Virtual employment

The driving forces that have motivated teleworking, remote locations and 'virtual offices', for example, are unlikely to go away. Traffic congestion will continue to increase and respect for the environment will become more important. Companies will need to attract better staff, improve customer service *and* reduce costs. Based on these facts, the amount of teleworkers or 'virtual office' staff is predicted to increase.

Predictions for the numbers of teleworkers vary widely, and to a large extent depend on the way teleworking is defined. It is estimated that the numbers of teleworkers in the year 2010 will be 10 million (UK) and 33 million (USA). This represents a significant proportion of the total workforce. In some types of work it will be much higher.

However, there will be no 'Teleworking Revolution'. What is more likely is an evolutionary change in working practices as a long-term result of the Information Technology Revolution. Teleworking will increasingly be absorbed into the mainstream of normal working practice. Organisations require greater flexibility to expand and contract their services to meet customer demand. This means longer opening hours and an ability to cope with peaks and troughs in demand. Using part-time and temporary workers can provide this flexibility. In addition, there will be more flexible working contracts, including job-sharing and teleworking.

The concept of what constitutes an office is changing. Traditional offices will be used in a more flexible way and offices will be developed where there will be no individual ownership of desk space. People who work in the building will have access to shared resources such as a telephone, terminal, meeting room, relaxation area. They will use these resources as appropriate when they are working in the office.

Technology will continue to improve. The bandwidths of digital communications links will continue to increase, allowing more information to be transmitted even quicker. Groupware, workflow management tools and schedulers will allow teams to be formed from people working in different places who will create 'virtual teams' and even 'virtual organisations'. The continuing developments and increasing availability of videotelephony is removing the social barriers of not being able to 'see' the person at the other end of the phone. Improved mobile communications and smaller, more powerful portable personal computers will make it easier to work wherever and whenever it suits – in the office, car, telecentre, hotel room, or at home. The office, with all its support systems, could be anywhere that the teleworker chooses.

As the nature of work and society continues to change, new places where work gets done will start to emerge. Rural areas are likely to see the development of 'televillages', communities in which people can both live and work in the information age. These televillages, growing from the concept of telecottages, will tackle the problems of housing and employment in rural areas, while making a positive contribution to the environment and quality of life.

Career planning action plan

- Keep your CV up-to-date.
- Maintain a journal of your significant achievements and projects.
- Network inside and outside of your organisation.
- Join, and actively attend, industry and professional organisations and associations.
- Stay in contact with previous school, college and work colleagues.
- Ask for unpaid leave to attend training courses.
- Work hard and put in extra effort where it will be noticed and reward yourself.
- Keep ahead of trends, look ahead five and ten years; anticipate change.
- Get your finances in order and ready for a 'rainy day'.
- Develop a 'work-for-yourself' attitude, do a good job, impress with competence, but remember that long hours and slavish devotion will not be rewarded automatically.
- Attend a training course, workshop or seminar once every three - six months; new learning and exchanging ideas keeps you alert and growing, even if the topics are non-work related.
- Always have a 'plan B'. 'If your job ended tomorrow, what would you do?'
- Invest a percentage of your income in training, study courses or educational books, tapes or videos; build a self-development library and constantly read and re-read key texts.
- Arrange social functions with friends and colleagues to share ideas and stay in touch.
- Start to save five or ten per cent of your monthly income.
- Stay ahead of technology – computers, software, and anything specific to your field, or an area that you would like to move into.
- Be ready to 'hustle' a job, without it being advertised.

- Work on smoothing out 'weak-spots' in your skills. This might be presentation skills, technical knowledge, time-keeping, financial awareness, etc.
- Consider all the options when you have to and keep an open mind to change.
- If you have to be a mercenary, then so be it. Find a job that pays well and gain personal fulfilment outside of your work.
- Consider becoming a freelancer. Organisations are quite used to using these in almost all areas of their operations – from the boardroom to the security lodge.
- Take-up golf, sailing or some other time-consuming leisure activity; you should work to live, not live to work.
- If you are aiming to stay in normal employment for a medium to large organisation, then you will need to learn the 'game' of success and survival. This means getting seen doing the right things, getting involved with the right projects, people and committees. The people who make it to the higher management positions are not the best performers, just the most successful 'politicians'.

Managing stress and anxiety

BEWARE...!
The stress at work and the boss might be killing you

Introduction to stress management: Reducing situation specific stress • Mood control

Stress and anxiety management

How to relieve stress at work

Avoiding burn-out: What is burn-out? • Symptoms Avoidance

Handling depression

Optimum stress levels: Understanding the importance of optimum stress levels • Finding your optimum stress levels

Eliminating stress from your environment

Anxiety: Mental energy

Stress reduction techniques: Stress management

Some healthful hints

And finally...

BEWARE...!
The stress at work and the boss might be killing you

Introduction to stress management: Reducing situation specific stress • Mood control

Stress and anxiety management

How to relieve stress at work

Avoiding burn-out: What is burn-out? • Symptoms Avoidance

Handling depression

Optimum stress levels: Understanding the importance of optimum stress levels • Finding your optimum stress levels

Eliminating stress from your environment

Anxiety: Mental energy

Stress reduction techniques: Stress management

Some healthful hints

And finally...

eleven

BEWARE...!

The stress at work and the boss might be killing you

While you daydream about strangling your boss, beware: it's more likely that your employer is killing you. Evidence can be found in numerous studies, including one undertaken with British civil servants, which suggest that the feeling of little or no control at work explains why employees have a 50 per cent higher risk of heart disease than the people in the executive suite.

The study published in *The Lancet* was directed by Professor Michael Marmot of the International Centre for Health and Society at University College, London. It used data from a study of 7,372 men and women employed in the British civil service who were tracked from 1985 to 1993.

Introduction to stress management

However, not all stress is bad for us. In fact, stress is something that is essential in certain situations. Although if we 'overload' ourselves or do not have adequate ways of recognising, reducing and recovering from it, stress can impair our performance in the short and long-term.

For our purposes here, there are basically two kinds of stress:

- Situation specific stress; anxiety or stress that is associated with a particular event or task.
- General or long-term stress build-up, often without a single, identifiable, source.

The stress, or anxiety associated with it, usually disappears when the task or event is over, but our ability and performance might suffer as a result. Secondly, more marginal affects are noticed in our behaviours or performance, which if left untreated or unrecognised, may lead to 'burn-out', depression or apathy.

Reducing situation specific stress

Removing event anxiety by achieving focus and flow

Achieving focus and flow is what 'peak performance' psychology is all about. It can be described as a state of complete concentration on performance – this is used and practised by almost all top sports professionals and athletes.

The qualities of 'flow' are as follows:

- aware of activities, but not aware of awareness
- high level of attention, focused completely on activity
- loss of self-consciousness, ego, evaluation, concern with results, judges, audience, other people's expectations
- in control of actions and reactions
- no voice or conscious decision making
- trust body to follow training
- altered state of consciousness: exhilarating
- feeling of omnipotence
- regulation of stream of consciousness to only relevant stimuli
- no attention paid to negative thinking, irrelevant sensory input, etc.

When do we need flow?

We can use flow whenever we have to perform at our best; when the stakes are high. Job interviews, presentations, exams, difficult tasks, technical work and so on.

Flow is fun and intrinsically rewarding

Achieving flow: flow can be achieved when your perceived ability to perform, matches perceived difficulty of performance.

Therefore seek to attain *performance goals*, not outcome goals – avoiding distractions eg criticism from others and completely focus on performance. This means no analysis and staying relaxed and alert. Top athletes and performers often develop routines and rituals, particularly using imagery to re-experience flow. You can only let flow happen – you cannot force it to happen.

Eliminating negative thoughts with positive thinking: the mind is programmed to detect and respond to (defensive, evolved reactions) – intense stimuli – noise, flashing light – movement – unusual stimuli – absence of usual stimuli – movement. In performance you may want to close out irrelevant stimuli.

Improving concentration/attention: analyse the attention demands of the task or job that you are doing – what skills require attention internally or externally – what situations require broad focus or narrow focus – learn how to switch between each – think positively – pay attention to what is happening now, not to past events.

Flow can be lost as we get better at something: our reactions become automatic and the task holds our attention less, especially where a specific outcome can be attained relatively easily – therefore allowing us to concentrate on performance goals and hold our concentration even when not challenging competition.

Improving focus: execute skill in practice then do it. Be aware of all around you then focus on you, do it by instinct – do not evaluate during an event. Create mental conditions of best performance and use reminders to enter the best state of mind. Start with a short period of focus, then expand to encompass the whole event.

Zen approach: oneness with self and task or activity. You should be totally present in activity, totally absorbed, no reflection, questioning, or attention to distraction, no desire for victory, desire to show off, wish to overawe enemy, desire to play passive role.

Things damaging to achievement of flow: stress, distraction, bad mood, bad mental energy management, evaluation of performance when you should just perform, concern with outcome.

Mood control

Bad mood: a bad mood affects our performance, damages focus and reduces motivation. Mood control can be achieved through positive thinking. Treat each element of an event or situation as separate from previous ones – so failure does not affect subsequent results. Feeling sluggish is just a mood. Counter your bad moods with positive suggestions.

Management of distraction: distraction is harmful as it damages flow and our ability to focus. Examples of distractions: thoughts, noise, relationships. When distracted, don't lose skills – just lose focus. Coping with distraction for a long time can lead to exhaustion and additional stress. Proper sleep and positive imagery can help.

Coping with distraction: know you can perform well despite distraction. Think positively. You can control your reaction to things beyond your control. Expect more distraction at bigger events. Practice refocusing when distracted. Learn how to change bad moods to good moods. At the end of a good or a bad event, draw out good points and be proud of them.

If feeling negative: find own space, regroup thoughts, refocus on goals, focus on something you enjoy. Positive self-image helps deal with distracting negative criticism.

Stress and anxiety management

Do not be afraid to frequently give yourself time to relax, to meditate or even to 'muck about'. But do so as a result of a conscious decision so that you can relax completely. Do not drift into periods of dawdling when you are half working and half resting.

Stress and anxiety management: this is the imbalance between perceived abilities and perceived requirements – where someone sees a task as too difficult – competition becomes a threat, not a challenge.

Roots of anxiety

1. A belief that you must always have the approval of all significant people. This is not true – some people are just disagreeable!
2. A belief that you must always be thoroughly competent. Everyone has bad days and makes mistakes. Enjoy them!
3. A belief that misery comes from external factors. Not true – this can often come from inside. Often 'bad' situations can be looked on positively. Bad people don't affect the intrinsic quality of your own performance.
4. A belief that people and events should always turn out the way that you want. People do what they want to do. People just are, the world just is.
5. A belief that the past always conditions you; 'I can change things if I work hard'.

Get at least ten minutes of programmed exercise every day, and throughout the day use every opportunity to walk, stand, climb stairs etc. This promotes health and also increases 'prime time' by reducing fatigue.

Recognising stress/arousal

Different people have different stress responses, but here are some general traits that you might notice:

Physical symptoms

- Heart rate up
- Blood pressure up
- Sweating up
- Brain waves up
- Urination up
- Adrenaline up
- Blood flow to skin down
- Cotton mouth

Mental symptoms

- Worry feeling
- Overwhelmed
- Inability to make decisions

Behavioural symptoms

- Rapid talking
- Nail biting
- Increased blinking
- Yawning
- Trembling broken voice

How to relieve stress at work

1. Take your 'emotional temperature'.

Ask yourself regularly, on a scale of 1-10 (1 being very calm and 10 being ready to jump off a building) 'How stressed am I?'

Giving yourself a number is a quick method of identifying, in your own terms, where you are emotionally. It is an early warning system. In my practice as a therapist, it constantly amazes me how many people go on from one day to the next without knowing that they are stressed until the discomfort becomes unbearable.

Taking your emotional temperature can give you a running start at catching your stress before it gets out of hand.

2. Take a break

Make sure you take a break that will re-energise you between 3pm and 4pm in the afternoon. That is the time that the body usually runs out of energy. If you just try and push past that period you will be more prone to make mistakes, get more frustrated, and even put unhealthy stress on your body.

3. Re-charge yourself

Take 'Re-energising Breaks' (R.B.), such as relaxing. (The best length of time to relax is 20 minutes, but if you can't do that, take what you can.) Even five minutes is better than not taking any time at all. Another example of an R.B. is a brisk walk. Research on productivity has shown that the time lost in taking an R.B. is more than made up for in effectiveness on the job. Remember how much time it takes to undo a mistake.

4. Pace yourself

If you have been doing a difficult task for a while, stop and take a break, unless you are on a roll. If possible, alternate tasks. Schedule a break for yourself before you run out of steam. Also, if you have been working on a challenging task for awhile think of doing a more routine one. The brain needs time to change gears.

You can push, but you will pay a price that might eventually be a high one.

5. Share a worry

Share that frustration with someone else, but be careful who you select. It may be best to talk to someone who you don't work with. Keeping things bottled up will also cause an explosion. If you need to immediately discharge the frustration, write down what and why you are frustrated. In the short-term, that may also relieve some pressure. If you are frustrated because you are angry with someone, write them a letter or a memo. Ultimately, you may not want to send them that communication, but in the short run it does get some of the frustration off your chest.

Ongoing stress has a measurable negative affect on individuals at work. It can cause or significantly contribute to physical, psychological and behavioural problems. Stress, whether related to job, home or other situations, can become 24-hour-a-day baggage with each 'stressor' compounding the others. For many workers, the effects of stress are amplified by smoking, alcohol and the use of drugs.

Here are some simple personal strategies for relieving, reducing and helping manage stress:

1. Relax and take time each day to do something 'fun'. This may include specifically dedicating a little personal time for 'doing nothing'.
2. Exercise – not only for fitness, but as a way of coping with 'stressors'.
3. Make humour part of your coping strategy. Laughter is a documented, demonstrated stress-relieving pressure valve.
4. Talk over the things that stress you. Don't hold them in. Let someone know how you feel. Sharing your feelings may very well yield a new slant on what's troubling you.
5. Get the sleep and rest that you need to function at your best level. Sometimes sleep and rest may seem like luxuries. Instead, they may provide the strength and clear-mindedness that you need to manage the stressful situation effectively.

Also, remember that the first step in reducing stress is taking the time to identify the specific things that are stressing you. You're much less likely to eliminate or reduce 'stressors' until you've figured out what they are, and why they affect you.

Avoiding burn-out

What is burn-out?

Burn-out occurs where people who have previously been highly committed to a task or activity lose interest and motivation. Typically it will occur in hard working, hard training, hard driven people who become emotionally, psychologically or physically exhausted. This can occur where:

- you find it difficult to say 'no' to additional commitments or responsibilities
- someone has been under intense and sustained pressure for some time
- someone is trying to achieve too much
- someone has been giving too much emotional support for too long.

Symptoms

Burn-out will normally occur slowly, over a long period of time. It may express itself physically or mentally. Symptoms of burn-out include:

- physical burn-out
- feelings of intense fatigue
- vulnerability to viral infection
- mental burn-out
- an incorrect belief that you are accomplishing less
- a growing tendency to think negatively
- loss of a sense of purpose and energy
- increasing detachment from relationships that cause conflict and stress, adding to burn-out.

Avoidance

If you are working hard, then you should take great care not to burn-out. You can avoid physical or mental burn-out by keeping the task or activity fun. You should, however, respect feelings of intense physical fatigue and rest appropriately. Likewise, there is a limit to your mental energy that you should respect. As you get better at a task or activity people will want more of your time and will rely on you more and more. You must learn to say 'No' to commitments that you do not want to take on – otherwise you will be in severe danger of burning-out as you become unhappy with your situation. Involvement in tasks must be fun, otherwise there is no point in doing them.

Are you in danger of burning-out?

If you feel that you are in danger of burning-out, or you are not enjoying life, the following points can help you correct the situation:

- Re-evaluate your goals and prioritise them
- Evaluate the demands placed on you and see how they fit in with your goals
- Identify your ability to comfortably meet these demands
- If you are over-involved, reduce the excessive commitments
- If people demand too much emotional energy, become more unapproachable and less sympathetic. Involve other people in a supportive role
- Learn and use stress management skills
- Examine other areas in your life which are generating stress, such as work or family, and try to solve problems and reduce the stress
- Get the support of your friends and family in reducing stress
- Ensure that you are following a healthy lifestyle
- Get adequate sleep and rest to maintain your energy levels
- Ensure that you are eating a healthy, balanced diet – a bad diet can make you ill
- Get adequate regular aerobic exercise

- Limit your caffeine and alcohol intake
- Perhaps develop alternative activities such as a relaxing hobby to take your mind off problems
- Acknowledge your own humanity: remember that you have a right to pleasure and a right to relaxation

Late stages of burn-out

If you are in the late stages of burn-out, feeling deeply demotivated and disenchanted with your task or activity, get help from a good friend. If you have burned-out do not worry. If you are so demotivated in your task or activity that for a time you do not want to continue, ease off for a while or even take an extended break. If you come back later, you may find that you start to enjoy it again, and can take on only those commitments you want to.

Plan 'If only...' days. 'If only I had time to...'

You may, however, find that you have absolutely no interest in continuing with the task or activity. In this case it is best to drop it altogether. If you are the sort of person who has burned-out, then a complete change of direction may be appropriate – it is very likely that you will find another area in which you will excel. You will find that you are only demotivated and listless in the area in which you burned-out.

The difference is that you will have already burned-out once: next time you will know the signs to look for and the things to watch. You will be able to pace yourself, and control your energy much more effectively, ensuring that you operate at stress levels where you can give your optimum performance.

Handling depression

Depression may often be initiated by high levels of long-term stress, by failure associated with stress-related under-performance, or by life crises. Deep depression is a clinical illness and should be treated medically. It is important that if you are depressed that you take this seriously. Severe depressions can cause years of unhappiness and low performance can be neutralised quickly with drugs, by the appropriate form of psychotherapy or by other forms of personal action. It is important to know when there is a problem, and when to ask for help.

Depression may start when:

- projects fail
- you are passed over for promotion
- you feel out of control
- you are very tired
- you are feeling inadequate while getting to grips with a new, difficult job
- you are bored for a long period of time.

The following points may help in handling depression before it gets serious:

An important way of guarding against depression is getting your attitude right, positive thinking really can help. As long as you can draw useful lessons from failure, then failure can be positive.

Similarly, talking about problems to a partner or to a respected colleague can often help a lot. They may have been through a similar situation, have seen the problem before or may be able to gently point out that you have the wrong perspective on a situation.

Effective time management can improve things when you are under stress as a result of excessive demands. Similarly taking an enjoyable break may reduce stress.

Where you are not under enough pressure, you can set personal challenges to increase stimulus. If you are already suffering from

a mild form of depression, then the following suggestions may help you to deal with it.

Self-confidence

Where lack of self-confidence is a factor, there are a number of things you can do:

Start to set personal goals. This will give you direction in life, and will help you to acknowledge that you can achieve useful and important things.

Write down a list of your negative points. Challenge each item on the list objectively, asking yourself 'Is this fair?', or 'Is this really serious?'. You should find that many of your negative beliefs are wrong or insignificant. Where you identify serious failings, set measurable personal goals to eliminate or neutralise them.

Similarly, bring your anxiety and negative self-talk up to the surface and consider them logically. Ask yourself whether it is realistic to worry about the things you worry about: if you have no control over them, then worry does no good. When you look at them, you may find that your worries are irrational or out of proportion.

Write down a list of the things that you can do well and the positive parts of your personality. Ignore 'virtues' like humility and modesty – these are not good for your self-confidence or well-being. Be proud of your good points – they can help you to contribute positively to the world.

Positive thinking. Almost all apparently negative experiences have positive elements to them. Learn to identify these positives: this will help you to draw the best from every situation. Even failing at something can be an intense and valuable learning experience.

Relationships

You may find that the root of problems lies with:

Assertiveness. If you are failing to assert yourself, you may find that other people are not paying attention to your wants and needs. This can be upsetting and humiliating. Learn to express your wishes firmly, but only be confrontational if absolutely necessary. Assertiveness training can be beneficial in learning to do this.

Social skills. If your relationships are difficult, then you may identify that difficulties lie in the way in which you deal with other people. Alternatively, if you can identify where things are going wrong, you may be able to set goals to overcome the problem.

Other people. It is easy to assume (especially when you are depressed) that the fault in relationship problems lies with you. This may or may not be the case. Examine your relationships rationally, you may find that people around you are causing problems. If people are making your life worse, then you may be better off without them.

Standards. You may find that you have set your standards unrealistically high. This will typically occur when you believe that a certain standard of achievement is necessary, and also when you do not have either the financial or time resources available to achieve those standards. In this case it may be realistic to assess the standards that you can reasonably achieve within the set constraints, and aim at these.

Fatigue and exhaustion. If you are very tired, or have been under stress for a long period, you may find that a good break helps you to put problems into perspective.

Optimum stress levels

Understanding the importance of optimum stress levels

This section explains the linkage between stress and performance, and shows how you can ensure that you perform at your best by optimising stress levels.

The level of stress under which you operate is important. If you are not under enough stress, then you may find that your performance suffers because you are bored and unmotivated. If you are under too much stress, then you will find that your results suffer as stress related problems interfere with your performance.

It is important to recognise that you are responsible for your own stress – very often it is a product of the way that you think. Learn to monitor your stress levels, and adjust them up if you need to be more alert, or down if you are feeling too tense. By managing your stress effectively you can significantly improve the quality of your life.

The approach to optimising stress depends on the sort of stress being experienced:

- Short-term stress such as presentations, meetings, interviews, or confrontational situations require the short-term management of adrenaline to maximise performance.
- Long-term stress, where fatigue and high adrenaline levels over a long period can lead to degraded performances, require concentration on the management of fatigue, health, energy and morale.

Naturally there is some element of overlap between short and long-term stress.

Short-term stress

The diagram below shows the relationship between stress and the quality of performance, when you are in situations that impose short-term stress.

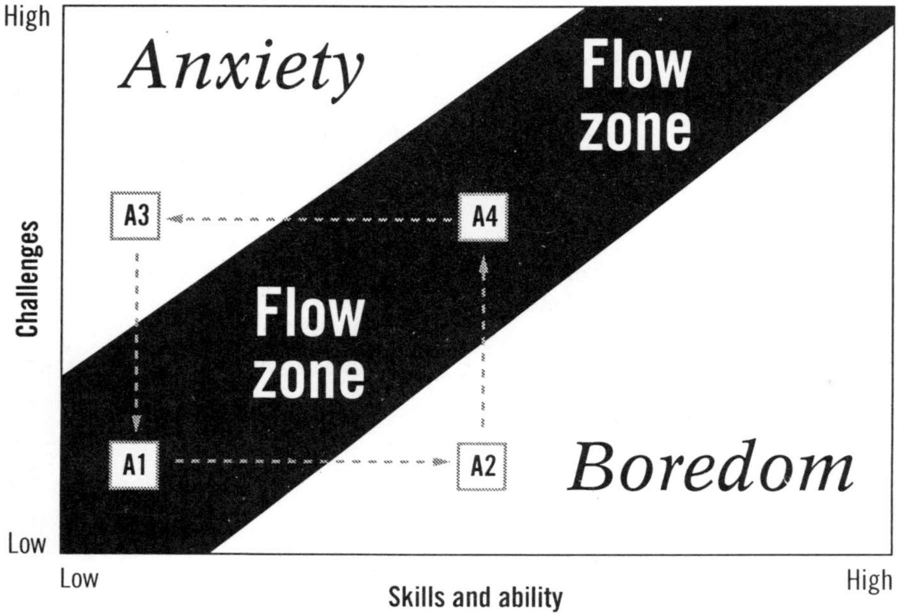

Figure 5: 'Flow' and optimum stress

Where stress is low, you may find that your performance is low because you become bored and lack concentration and motivation.

Where stress is too high, your performance can suffer from all the symptoms of short-term stress.

In the middle, at a moderate level of stress, there is a zone of best performance. If you can keep yourself within this zone, then you will be sufficiently aroused to perform well while not being over-stressed and unhappy.

This graph, and this zone of optimum performance are different shapes for different people. Some people may operate most effectively at a level of stress that would leave other people either bored or in pieces. It is possible that someone who functions superbly at a low level might experience difficulties at a high level. Alternatively, someone who performs only moderately at low level might perform exceptionally under extreme pressure.

Long-term stress

The problems of long-term, sustained stress, are more associated with fatigue, morale and health than with short-term adrenaline management.

There are four major stages that you may go through in response to sustained levels of excessive stress:

- During the first phase you will face challenges with plenty of energy. Your response will probably be positive and effective.
- After a period of time you may begin to feel seriously tired. You may start to feel anxious, frustrated and upset. The quality of your work may begin to suffer.
- As high stress continues you may begin to feel a sense of failure and may be ill more frequently. You may also begin to feel exploited by your organisation. At this stage you may begin to distance yourself from your employer, perhaps starting to look for a new job.
- If high levels of stress continue without relief you may ultimately experience depression, burnout, nervous breakdown, or some other form of serious stress related illness.

Different people may move between these stages with varying speed according to the stress conditions.

At a simple level it may appear that a measure of 'toughness' is how well you keep on going under extreme stress. This is simplistic. It is certainly possible to be self-indulgent and use stress as an excuse for not pushing yourself hard enough. It is, however, also far too easy to let yourself be pushed to a level where your work, as well as your physical and mental health, start to suffer. The strongest and most flexible position is to actively manage your levels of stress and fatigue so that you are able to produce high quality work over a long period, reliably.

High performance in your job may require continued hard work in the face of high levels of sustained stress. If this is the case, it is essential that you learn to pay attention to your feelings. This ensures that you know when to relax, slacken off for a short period, get more sleep or implement stress release strategies. If you do not take feelings of tiredness, upset or discontent seriously, then you may face failure, burn-out or breakdown.

As well as paying attention to your own stress levels, it may be worth paying attention to the stress under which people around you operate. If you are a manager seeking to improve productivity, then failing to monitor stress may mean that you drive employees into depression or burn-out. If this is a danger, then reduce stress for long enough for them to recover, and then reconsider the pace you are setting.

Finding your optimum stress levels

The best way of finding your optimum level of stress is to keep a note of whenever you feel 'stressed' in your diary for a number of weeks, also noting other events or thoughts at the time.

Eliminating stress from your environment

If your living and working environments are badly organised then they can be a major source of stress. If your environment is well organised and pleasant, then it can help to reduce stress and increase productivity. Remember though that, while it may be important for people under stress to have a calm environment, others may enjoy the raised levels of arousal associated with the 'buzz' of a busy office, or non-routine lifestyle.

While the points listed may each contribute in only a small way to creating a more pleasant environment, taken together they can have a significant effect in reducing stress. This section explains how you can reduce stress in your environment by improving:

- Air quality
- Lighting
- Decoration and tidiness
- Noise
- Furniture and ergonomics
- Personal space

Air quality

Poor air quality can make life unpleasant. Smoking, over-crowding and heating can contribute to the problem.

You can do a number of things to improve air quality and reduce the stress caused by it:

- Ban smoking
- Open windows
- Use an ioniser to freshen the air by eliminating positive ions created by eg electric motors powering computer fans
- Use dehumidifiers where humidity is a problem
- Introduce plants where the air is too dry. Evaporation of water from the plant pots or from the plants themselves will help to raise humidity. Plants also raise the amount of oxygen in the air and reduce stuffiness.

Lighting

Bad lighting can cause eye strain and increase fatigue, as can light that is too bright, or light that shines directly into your eyes. Fluorescent lighting can also be tiring. What you may not appreciate is that the quality of light may also be important. Most people are happiest in bright sunshine – this may cause release of chemicals in the body that bring a feeling of emotional well-being. Artificial light, which typically comprises only a few wavelengths of light, does not seem to have the same effect on mood that sunlight has. Try experimenting with working by a window or using full spectrum bulbs in your desk lamp. You will probably find that this improves the quality of your working environment.

Decoration and tidiness

If your environment at work or home is dirty, uncomfortable or neglected, then this can cause stress. Similarly, if your living or working area is untidy and chaotic, then this can be distracting. It is important, however, not to be dogmatic about tidiness: while it is very difficult to successfully co-ordinate many tasks in an untidy work area, it is perfectly possible to work on one task successfully. One of the most important lessons about human beings is that people work in different ways.

Noise

Noise can cause intense stress. In a working environment, a high level of background noise can severely impair your ability to concentrate. In an open plan office, the sound of people talking casually, of office machinery or of meetings going on can seriously undermine the quality of work done. Ringing telephones disturb not only the person to whom the call is directed, but also other people in the same area. Large amounts of background noise during the day can cause irritability, tension and headaches in addition to loss of concentration. Solutions to noise at work can involve:

- installation of partitions
- use of meeting rooms separate from the main work area
- use of quiet rooms when concentration is needed
- and, if all else fails, use of earplugs or a personal stereo.

In a home environment, unwanted noise can be even more stressful and irritating as it intrudes on private space. Where noise comes from neighbours or someone sharing the house, it may be effective to try a pleasantly assertive approach. Ask that music is turned down or that a different room be used as a child's nursery. Where noise comes from outside the home, double glazing may be effective in reducing it.

Furniture and ergonomics

Another source of stress is muscular tension and pain caused by poorly designed furniture, or by inappropriate use of good furniture. It is important to take the time to arrange your working environment so that it is comfortable. For example, when you consider that you may spend a large proportion of each day sitting in a particular seat, it is worth ensuring that it is not causing you pain or damaging your body. If you work at a computer, then ensure that the monitor and keyboard are comfortably positioned, and that you are well-positioned relative to them. If you find that tendons in your hands get sore when you type for sustained periods, then it may be worth experimenting with a 'natural' keyboard.

If you find that your eyes get sore when looking at a monitor, or that you get headaches, then try taking breaks periodically. If you feel that you are experiencing pain from your environment, it may be worth looking into ergonomics in more detail.

Personal space

It is important for people to feel that they have sufficient personal space at work and at home. You may have experienced the dissatisfaction, stress and irritation of working at a different desk each day, or of sleeping in a different hotel room each night. This unpleasant situation is largely caused by the lack of power to organise and control the space in which you operate. Other people can also cause you stress when they impose themselves on your personal space, perhaps entering it uninvited.

The ideal way of establishing personal space is to have a room or office of your own, into which you control access. If this is not possible, you can block off areas with furniture, screens or blinds. In the highly undesirable situation where no personal space is available, then you can establish some feeling of ownership by bringing personal objects such as small plants or photographs of loved-ones into the workspace.

Some recent experiments in management practice have involved eliminating personal space in the working environment, allocating different working cubicles to members of staff each time they come in. This can work well, but not for everybody.

Anxiety

Anxiety is different from stress. Anxiety comes from a concern over lack of control over circumstances. In some cases being anxious and worrying over a problem may generate a solution. Normally, however, it will just result in negative thinking.

Mental energy

You need mental energy to be able to concentrate your attention and maintain good mental attitudes. If you are concentrating effectively then you can conserve physical energy by maintaining good techniques when your muscles are tired, can maintain focus and good execution of skills, and can push and drive your body through pain and fatigue barriers.

You can waste mental energy on worry, stress, fretting over distractions, and negative thinking. Over a long period these not only damage enjoyment, but also drain energy so that performance suffers.

It is therefore important to avoid these by good use of 'peak performance' psychology, and by relaxing effectively and by ensuring that you sleep properly, and for long enough.

Stress reduction techniques

This area demonstrates methods of reducing stress to a level where you can perform more effectively. The techniques that you select depend on the cause of the stress and the situation in which the stress occurs.

In choosing methods to combat stress, it is worth asking yourself where the stress comes from: if outside factors such as job or relationship difficulties are causing stress, then a positive thinking or imagery based technique may be effective. If the stress is based on the feeling of adrenaline in the body, then it may be effective purely to relax the body and slow the flow of adrenaline.

As with all 'peak performance' psychology skills, the effectiveness of the stress reduction technique depends on practice.

Stress management

Many people don't realise it, but stress is a very natural and important part of life. Without stress there would be no life at all! We need stress (eustress), but not too much stress for too long (distress). Our body is designed to react to both types of stress. Eustress helps keep us alert, motivates us to face challenges, and drives us to solve problems. These low levels of stress are manageable and can be thought of as necessary and normal stimulation.

What we all need to do is learn how to approach matters in more realistic and reasonable ways. Strong reactions are better reserved for serious situations. Manageable reactions are better for the everyday issues that we all have to face.

Some healthful hints

Basically, we need to modify our over-reactions to situations. Rather than seeing situations as psychologically or physically threatening and thereby activating our sympathetic nervous system, our parasympathetic nervous system (that part which helps lower physiological arousal) needs to be called into play. The following suggestions are designed to reduce distress. Try them. They work!

1. Learn to relax

- Throughout the day, take 'minibreaks' Sit-down and get comfortable, slowly take a deep breath in, hold it, and then exhale very slowly. At the same time, let your shoulder muscles droop, smile, and say something positive like, 'I am r-e-l-a-x-e-d.'
- Be sure to get sufficient rest at night. Once a week be in bed by 9pm.
- In traffic or when travelling, stay calm and physically relaxed, listen to classical music.
- Go on a news-fast for a whole week. No radio, TV, and especially no newspapers. Instead read quality books, draw, play an instrument, paint, listen to music or just do nothing!

2. Practice acceptance

- Many people get distressed over things they won't let themselves accept. Often these are things that can't be changed, like someone else's feelings or beliefs.
- If something unjust bothers you, that is different. If you act in a responsible way, the chances are you will manage stress effectively.
- Don't try and change others – change yourself.
- Remember, we cannot control what happens to us in life, only how we react to it.
- Take responsibility for your own thoughts and actions.
- Resist judging people, things or events as 'bad' or 'good' – things just '*are*'.

- When something 'bad' happens, immediately imagine how much worse it might have been and 'Well it's lucky that....'
- When you find yourself doing or experiencing something pleasant or of importance – whether it is a beautiful sunset or meeting with friends – slow down and enjoy the moment by immersing yourself 100 per cent in the 'now'.

3. Talk rationally to yourself

- Ask yourself what real impact the stressful situation will have on you in a day or a week and see if you can let the negative thoughts go.
- Think whether the situation is your problem or the other persons. If it is yours, approach it calmly and firmly; if it is the other persons, there is not much you can do about it.
- Rather than condemn yourself with hindsight thinking like, 'I should have...,' think about what you can learn from the error and plan for the future.
- Watch out for perfectionism – set realistic and attainable goals.
- Remember, everyone makes mistakes. Be careful of procrastination – breaking tasks into smaller units will help and prioritising will help get things done.

4. Get organised

- Develop a realistic schedule of daily activities that includes time for work, sleep, relationships and recreation.
- Use a daily To-do list – at work and at home.
- Improve your physical surroundings by cleaning your house and straightening up your work area or office.
- Use your time and energy as efficiently as possible.
- Regularly turn-out cupboards and storage to clear out clutter.
- Get all your finances in order – get in the black and stay there.
- Simplify everything, eliminate trivia, throw more away.

5. Exercise

- Physical activity has always provided relief from stress. In the past, daily work was largely physical, now that physical exertion is no longer a requirement for earning a living, we don't get rid of stress so easily while working. It accumulates very quickly.
- Develop a regular exercise programme to help reduce the effects of working.
- Try aerobics, walking, jogging, dancing, swimming, anything that gets your pulse above resting.
- Take a brisk 20 minute walk whenever you can.
- Build activity into your day – take the stairs not lifts, park further from your work, go for a swim or a walk in your lunch break.

6. Reduce time urgency

- If you frequently check your watch or worry about what you do with your time, learn to take things a bit slower.
- Allow plenty of time to get things done.
- Plan your schedule ahead of time.
- Instead of trying to 'cram' everything into your day – ask others to help or do less.
- Recognise that you can only do so much in a given period.
- Practice the notion of 'pace, not race.'
- Go on a 'clock-free weekend' – take down all clocks and don't wear a watch. Get-up, eat, shop, etc when you want to and for as long as you want. Experience time – don't be ruled by it.

7. Disarm yourself

- Every situation in life does not require you to be competitive. Adjust your approach to an event according to its demands. Playing tennis with a friend doesn't have to be an Olympic trial.
- You don't have to raise your voice in a simple discussion.
- Leave behind you 'weapons' of shutting out, having the last word, putting someone else down, and blaming.
- You don't have to be right.
- You have nothing to prove.
- There is no-one in the world better or worse than you; only you are you – and you are perfect.
- You are not your car, house or the clothes you wear.
- Sometimes the best thing you can do is to literally 'Let go' of your goals, dreams and especially the expectations of others and just be, do and think whatever and wherever life takes you.
- Don't feel guilty for spending your own time your own way; for leaving work on time or even early if you have achieved your main objectives; for taking and making time for you – you are worth it.

8. Quiet time

- Balance your family, social and work demands with special private times.
- Hobbies are good antidotes for daily pressures.
- Unwind by taking a quiet stroll, soaking in a hot bath, reading, drawing, watching a sunset, or listening to music.
- On a daily basis, sit quietly for at least 20 minutes and do nothing. Close your eyes and just let your thoughts go where ever they will.
- Keep a diary or journal to record your day or observations in.
- Before bed, take a long hot bath with just candle light – this is a wonderful way to relax.

9. Watch your habits. Eat sensibly

- A balanced diet will provide all the necessary energy you will need during the day.
- Avoid non-prescription drugs and minimise your alcohol use – you need to be mentally and physically alert to deal with stress.
- Be mindful of the effects of excessive caffeine and sugar on nervousness. Cut out the cigarettes – they restrict blood circulation and affect the stress response.
- Drink plenty of water – at least six glasses a day.
- Eat five or more portions of fruit or vegetables a day.
- Skip the occasional meal, and fast for a day, eating only fruit and drinking juices.

10. Talk to friends

- Friends can be good medicine. Daily doses of conversation, regular social engagements, and occasional sharing of deep feelings and thoughts can reduce stress quite nicely.
- Pick up the phone, share a problem and a pleasure 'It's good to talk.'

And finally...

This is taken from the crypt of Westminster Abbey. It is the inscription on the tomb of an Anglican Bishop.

'When I was young and free and my imagination had no limits.

I dreamed of changing the world.

As I grew older and wiser I discovered the world would not change

So I shortened my sights somewhat and decided to change only my country.

But it too seemed immovable.

As I grew into my twilight years, in one last desperate attempt

I settled for changing only my family, those closest to me.

But alas they would have none of it.

And now as I lay on my deathbed

I suddenly realise if only I had changed myself first

then by example I would have changed my family,

from their inspiration and encouragement I

would have been able to better my country

who knows I may have even changed the world'

Go on – take a break ...
...you deserve it!